Praise for *Make Work W*

A game-changer for anyone looking to thrive at work!

This book couldn't have come at a better time. It's full of practical insights that resonate deeply with today's work culture. It's all about finding a balance between personal well-being and professional success—something we're all trying to master.

Louise brings a unique focus on combining performance, growth, and well-being, making it essential reading for CEOs, founders, and leaders. It's a funny, insightful, and very relatable read! Highly recommended for anyone who wants to rethink their relationship with work.

CHAD STEPHENS, 2x Exited Founder, Startup Advisor and Angel Investor

Bridging the gap between research and reality

As a work-life researcher, I'm constantly seeking insights that resonate both intellectually and emotionally. Louise Gilbert's *Make Work Work for You* delivers exactly that. The relatable anecdotes, like the overwhelmed leader who unknowingly perpetuated a culture of dependency, hit home and highlight the often-unseen dynamics that shape our workplaces. The 'Three Pedals of Excellence' model provides a practical framework for achieving sustainable success, reminding us that it's not about work or life, but rather work and life in harmony. This book is a must-read for anyone seeking to create a fulfilling and balanced life, both personally and professionally.

CARYS CHAN, Senior Lecturer, Griffith University

A terrific read, full of great ideas

Louise Gilbert's *Make Work Work for You*, hits the nail on the head—having the right culture is fundamental to achieving high performance.

The book challenges us to think to create intentional environments to foster the culture we want. I particularly love the idea of organising 'f***ed-up nights'

As a CEO, I have always tried to foster a 'no-blame' and 'safe-to-fail' culture, but I had never thought of hosting 'f***ed-up nights'!!

Overall, a terrific read—full of great ideas—highly recommend.

PHILLIP RIPPER, CEO, No to Violence

Authentic and caring leadership

Louise's book couldn't have come at a better time. *Make Work Work for You* speaks to the heart of what it means to lead with authenticity and care. Louise's practical advice on balancing performance, growth, and wellbeing feels like a breath of fresh air. It's not just about achieving success at work but about showing up as our true, healthy selves every day. This guide is more than just a tool—it's a genuine support for leaders who want to navigate the challenges of today's workplace with both strength and heart. Thank you for addressing such a crucial need, Louise.

JAMES LOLICATO, Chief Operating Officer, Mancave

Transformative insights for modern leadership
Louise Gilbert's *Make Work Work for You* is a game-changer for anyone striving to redefine their work experience. This book not only provides a fresh perspective on work but also equips you with actionable strategies to elevate your leadership and team dynamics.

What truly stands out is how Louise's approach resonates on a personal level. I found the practical insights and the emphasis on balancing performance, growth, and wellbeing to be incredibly impactful. It's a brilliant guide for leaders who want to foster a more engaged and productive team while also prioritizing individual fulfillment.

The concepts are both thought-provoking and highly relatable, making it a must-read for anyone looking to transform their professional environment. This book has given me the tools to drive positive change within my organization and truly make work work for everyone involved.

BRENTON RICHMOND, General Manager, Inghams Enterprises Pty Ltd

Practical tips to improve your work life

The state of the modern workplace is troubling: we're consistently stressed, unhappy, and burned out. Given the incredible increases in worker productivity and GDP per capita over the last 200 years, it seems positive progress is being made everywhere in the workplace except in the human experience of it.

Enter Louise Gilbert, and *Make Work Work for You*. Louise understands humans. She knows how we think, how we feel, and how we operate in the modern world, and in this book, she unpacks twenty-seven (yes, twenty-seven!) practices that each have the potential to dramatically improve how we feel about work, and positively impact the contributions we make. I defy anyone not to find at least one practical tip to improve your work life in this book.

COL FINK, Business Coach, Author of *Speakership*, *Tribe of Learning* and *The Solo Pro*

MAKE
WORK
WORK
FOR
YOU

MAKE WORK WORK FOR YOU

27 Leadership Practices to Achieve Excellence across Performance, Growth and Wellbeing

LOUISE GILBERT

GRAMMAR
FACTORY
— EST? 2013 —

Published by Grammar Factory Publishing, an imprint of MacMillan
Company Limited.

Grammar Factory Publishing
MacMillan Company Limited
25 Telegram Mews, 39th Floor, Suite 3906
Toronto, Ontario, Canada
M5V 3Z1

www.grammarfactory.com

Louise Gilbert.
Make Work Work for You: 27 Leadership Practices to Achieve Excellence
across Performance, Growth and Wellbeing / Louise Gilbert.

Paperback ISBN 978-1-998756-93-3
eBook ISBN 978-1-998756-94-0
Audiobook ISBN 978-1-998528-08-0

1. BUS071000 BUSINESS & ECONOMICS / Leadership.
2. BUS085000 BUSINESS & ECONOMICS / Organizational Behavior.
3. BUS107000 BUSINESS & ECONOMICS / Personal Success.

PRODUCTION CREDITS
Cover design by Designerbility
Interior layout design by Setareh Ashrafologhalai
Book production and editorial services by Grammar Factory Publishing

GRAMMAR FACTORY'S CARBON NEUTRAL PUBLISHING COMMITMENT
Grammar Factory Publishing is proud to be neutralizing the carbon foot-
print of all printed copies of its authors' books printed by or ordered
directly through Grammar Factory or its affiliated companies through the
purchase of Gold Standard-Certified International Offsets.

*To Elodie—you're my new pair of
glasses through which I see the world. x*

(I love you too, Harrison.)

CONTENTS

INTRODUCTION 1

GUIDE TO THE PRACTICES 11

PART 1 **INDIVIDUAL PRACTICES**

INDIVIDUAL WELLBEING 19
Work/life contamination 21
Work/life whiplash 31
Work/life wealth 41

INDIVIDUAL GROWTH 49
Build change-making energy 51
Drive your development 61
Build Mindset X 69

INDIVIDUAL PERFORMANCE 79
Know your stress language 81
Honour needs, not norms 89
Manage your state 97

PART 2 **TEAM PRACTICES**

TEAM WELLBEING 111
Team tetris 113
Meeting makeovers 123
Quick, quality chats 131

TEAM GROWTH   139

Give (good) feedback;
get (good) feedback   141

Learn together; grow together   151

Notice the noise; find the need   159

TEAM PERFORMANCE   167

Aligned purpose   169

Great relationships   177

Clear roles   185

PART 3 **ORGANISATION
PRACTICES**

ORGANISATION WELLBEING   199

Built-in wellbeing   201

Human-centric change   209

Powerful engagement   217

ORGANISATION GROWTH   225

Look before you leap   227

Be constantly curious   237

Guide your growth   245

**ORGANISATION
PERFORMANCE   259**

Take off and transform   261

Cultivate your culture   275

Mine some metaphors   283

CONCLUSION:
MAKING WORK WORK FOR YOU
NOW AND IN THE FUTURE 293

ACKNOWLEDGEMENTS 301

INTRODUCTION

WHEN I WAS seventeen, my dad, Vince, and my big brother, Chris, were adamant I needed to learn to drive a manual car. 'Don't even bother with an automatic, Louise,' was their advice. I was wary of the whole idea—three pedals? Yikes! Why make it harder for me? What if I pressed the wrong pedal at the wrong time? Sounded like a disaster waiting to happen. But Chris convinced me by saying it'd be easier to get a boyfriend. This was the early 2000s, and being able to drive a sportscar was impressive, according to my brother. Wearing braces and being at an all-girls school, I was aware of my chances of getting a boyfriend, so I listened to him.

Next thing I knew, we jumped in Chris's car and headed down to the local beach, Half Moon Bay, where there was a huge ramp leading down towards the sea. Chris drove halfway up the ramp, turned the car off, and then told me to switch seats with him and drive the rest of the way. I was being chucked into the deep end and had to sink or swim. Literally. If I released the clutch too quickly I'd stall the car and my brother and I would slide down the hill into the murky depths of the bay below.

And that's how I learnt to drive a manual. How to press the right pedal at the right time.

In business, you also have three pedals—performance, growth and wellbeing. **Wellbeing** is about feeling good. It's a state where you feel purposeful and engaged and have healthy relationships. This applies not just to you but to your team and the whole organisation. **Growth** is about getting better. It's about personal and professional skills and capacity. Teams and organisations also experience growth. It's about change and about becoming *more*. **Performance** is about doing great. It's getting the job done, reaching the outcome, and reaping the benefits.

If you're not pressing the right pedals at the right times, your organisation may not be able to achieve excellence, and some of this might sound familiar...

- Your people are stressed and on the verge of burnout.

- You're having trouble attracting, retaining and developing the right people.

- Your teams struggle to work well together, especially in the hybrid work scenario.

- There's more work than your teams can handle.

Performance, growth and wellbeing are critical elements that you, your teams and your organisation need to achieve excellence and make work work for you. They reinforce each other. You can't have one without the other. It's about feeling good AND doing great AND getting better. When you have one or two of these things but not the second and third, you're out of whack. When you're out of whack— when you're hitting the wrong pedal at the wrong time, or just one or two but not all three—work won't work for you.

You may remember a time when organisations were all about growth and performance. Back then, growing fast was the goal. We threw everything we had into maximising profits, getting market share, and becoming the go-to people for whatever widgets we were making. We had to be the biggest and the brightest. Then, after a few years we wondered why everybody was going to bed for months on end or giving up the rat race to sit on top of a mountain and meditate for the rest of their lives. Burnout became an epidemic and everybody was jumping ship.

All the leaders went, 'Oh God, we need to prioritise wellbeing.' So, we shifted our focus over to that pedal. We sent people to retreats and spas. We did a bunch of stuff that made us feel really good. Inevitably, performance suffered because we took our foot off that pedal. Then we put our foot back on the performance pedal, and guess what? Six months later, everybody's burnt out again. It became a vicious cycle.

When you have growth and performance, you have **acceleration**. But you see the problem here... Without wellbeing, acceleration is **unsustainable**.

When you have growth and wellbeing, there is **evolution**. You're moving forward and developing. There's progress. However, unless you include performance in the mix, the organisation will be **unviable.** Shareholders have to be kept happy, and profits have to be made. You can innovate your socks off, but if nobody is buying your whizz-bang new products and they just sit on the shelf, the organisation will die.

When you have wellbeing and performance, you have **consistency**, but without growth, you will remain **underdeveloped.** This is when stagnation sets in. In today's market, where competition is fierce, customers need change and want more. Without an innovative edge, an organisation will soon become irrelevant.

FIGURE 1 3 Pedals of Excellence

Excellence is found around the edges

The problem is that people think of these three things as zero-sum. They accept the belief that if you push on the performance pedal, the other two might come down. Or if you focus on growth for a while, that will come at the expense of performance. There's this sense of bargaining and trading off... of haggling or fighting... of compromise. We need to reduce the friction between these three areas and create flow and alignment between them both inside and outside these realms and in the spaces where they meet. Excellence is in the edges.

It is possible to achieve performance, growth and wellbeing in equal measure. To feel good, do great and get better. The key is knowing how to push on the three pedals in ways that are positive sum. To push the right pedal at the right time. To push on one pedal without backing off on one or both of the others. And there are ways to do this that will help you improve across all three areas. It's not a trade-off. It's plus, plus, plus.

Performance + Growth + Wellbeing
means an individual, team or
organisation is accelerating and
evolving consistently.
This is business excellence.

Formula 1 is a sport dedicated to the relentless pursuit of excellence. It's cutting edge. This pursuit of excellence means cars now reach speeds of almost 400 kilometres per hour. But even Formula 1 has to find balance. When I interviewed F1 commentator David Croft about this, he explained how the wellbeing of teams couldn't simply be brushed aside to accommodate the voracious appetite of the public for more and faster races. Mechanics have to sleep. Drivers need time off. Nowadays, there are curfews, and teams sleep in comfortable hotel rooms, not in the paddock behind the team garage. And these changes have made a material difference. In 1994, Ayrton Senna became the twenty-ninth F1 driver to be killed in either practice or racing. But in the thirty years since, there has been only one death. That is one death too many, and improvements in safety continue, but the cars are faster than ever. It's all about finding the balance that allows excellence to emerge.

As a leader, you need to work out how to do things so that you're improving your performance, increasing your growth and enhancing your wellbeing simultaneously. You need strategies to help you do that. And that is what this book is all about. *Making Work Work for You* presents twenty-seven practices leaders can use to ensure their people are feeling good, doing great and getting better. These are the practical moves leaders can make that will help balance performance, growth and wellbeing while achieving excellence.

It's a bit like a Twister game. If you haven't played it ... There's a mat with coloured circles, and spinning a wheel tells you to put your left foot or your right foot or one of your hands on a red circle, a blue circle, a green circle or a yellow circle. The trick is doing this without becoming unbalanced. Work is like this. If wellbeing is suffering, you need to get a hand or a foot on a wellbeing circle, but you must do this without the whole organisation becoming unbalanced. If all your employees go meditate on a mountain for a year, the company will end up in the ditch. You need to find a way to enhance wellbeing without sending the company broke—find a circle on the Twister mat that's the right colour and won't tip you over as you reach for it. The practices in this book are like those coloured circles. Choose a circle to reach for that won't tip you over but will keep you balanced and upright.

In this book, I bring together lessons from hundreds of organisations. These key leadership practices will foster performance, growth and wellbeing for individuals, teams and organisations. I've wrapped up everything I know about inspiring change, creating real shifts, achieving transformational outcomes and bringing all this together in the day-to-day. Working the right way fuels our performance, helps us grow and builds our wellbeing. And while each practice in this book focuses on one area, if you apply them diligently you will find that they enhance all three. Everything is connected. Excellence is contagious. It's found in the spaces where all three areas meet. Together, these practices will make work work for you.

How to use this book

I'd love it if you could read my book cover to cover and absorb all the lessons presented here. But I've been working in the field of change for almost two decades now, and I know how it works; I get that you're busy. So, start small. Start tiny. Give one practice a go and embed it before you move on to another. I've deliberately designed this book so you can pick it up, put it down, practise one practice and then pick it up again. I hope to see photos of readers holding well-thumbed, dog-eared books that have been put to good use.

Each practice is designed to help you press one of the three pedals of excellence—performance, growth and wellbeing—and is further classified into the areas of individual, team and organisation. On page 11, you'll see the twenty-seven practices set out in a grid to help you find one that meets your most pressing needs.

Let's say you're concerned about how work is affecting your individual wellbeing. If you look at the grid, you'll find three practices listed under the intersection of 'wellbeing' and 'individual', plus a description that extracts the essence of what that practice is about. That will help you choose which one to try out. Or maybe you're concerned about the performance of the organisation as a whole. In that case, look up the practices under the intersection of 'performance' and 'organisation'. And so on. None of the twenty-seven leadership practices is a long-winded essay. I've kept things short and sweet so you can get the gist of what I'm talking about and quickly put the practices into—well—practice.

And here's the kicker—while each practice powers one pedal, they're strengthening the other two as well! These practices do not require you to make trade-offs between your performance and wellbeing. They show you how to make the right moves at the right time to create excellence. For example, knowing your stress language so you can do something about it is under 'wellbeing.' But this isn't just good for your health and wellbeing. It boosts your performance and supports your personal and professional growth.

As you begin to deploy more of these practices, you'll begin to absorb the lessons and find that you reach for them automatically when you need to push on a particular pedal. Over time, these twenty-seven lessons will begin to merge, and their combined effect will become greater than the power of the individual practices. Your improved expertise and your ability to change the way you think will set you up for the challenges of an uncertain future and propel you to greater success as a leader who knows how to make work work for you and your organisation.

I've spent close to twenty years as a change consultant and have worked with thousands of people and over a hundred organisations. I'm a speaker, facilitator and mentor, and I develop, train and coach at the executive, team and individual levels. I understand the interplay of performance, growth and wellbeing, as well as when and how to apply the strategies in each area to achieve excellence. I'm also a start-up founder, entrepreneur and business owner, and I know firsthand the challenges that leaders face. My experience is underpinned by education and lifelong learning, and at the last count I've undertaken twenty-eight licences, certifications and short courses—a dedication to learning I'd like to thank my neurodivergent brain for! So, trust me when I say I know how to make work work for you.

I hope this book will change your view of the world of work. I hope that you will learn that there is no need to compromise on performance, growth or wellbeing. With these twenty-seven practices as your starting point, you can embrace a future dedicated to striving for excellence. This book will help you feel less smashed and less stressed and enable you to lead a better life while achieving big improvements and outcomes in your business. Whether you're a seasoned executive or an aspiring leader, in these pages you will find the tools you need to thrive in the modern workplace and make work truly work for you.

GUIDE TO
THE PRACTICES

THE FOLLOWING tables will help you navigate the twenty-seven practices. They allow you to quickly find the practice that will best support your specific needs using the questions listed.

	INDIVIDUAL	TEAM	ORGANISATION
WELLBEING FEELING GOOD	• Work/life contamination (p21) • Work/life whiplash (p31) • Work/life wealth (p41)	• Team tetris (p113) • Meeting makeovers (p123) • Quick, quality chats (p131)	• Built-in wellbeing (p201) • Human-centric change (p209) • Powerful engagement (p217)
GROWTH DOING GREAT	• Build change-making energy (p51) • Drive your development (p61) • Build Mindset X (p69)	• Give (good) feedback; get (good) feedback (p141) • Learn together; grow together (p151) • Notice the need; find the noise (p159)	• Look before you leap (p227) • Constant curiosity (p237) • Guided growth (p245)
PERFORMANCE GETTING BETTER	• Know your stress language (p81) • Honour needs, not norms (p89) • Manage your state (p97)	• Aligned purpose (p169) • Great relationships (p177) • Clear roles (p185)	• Take off and transform (p261) • Cultivate your culture (p275) • Mine some metaphors (p283)

Part 1—Individual practices

Work/life contamination	Is your work poisoning your life?	**p21**
	This practice will help you find a cure.	
Work/life whiplash	Are the clashing demands of work and life clamouring for your attention, making it impossible to focus effectively?	**p31**
	This practice will teach you how to handle competing demands and protect yourself from serious 'injury'.	
Work/ life wealth	Do you long for a better work/life balance? Do you wish you had more time to actually live your life?	**p41**
	This practice will get you started on creating the life you want, one that feels good and has no regrets.	
Build change-making energy	Are you stuck in a rut? Do you want to make changes but find you keep falling at the first hurdle?	**p51**
	This practice will help you find the energy that's been missing.	
Drive your development	Do you have a development plan? Maybe. But how do you feel when you look at it? Energised and excited? Or bored because it was a TICK AND FLICK?	**p61**
	This practice will explain how to create a development plan that lights you up.	
Build Mindset X	Can you deal confidently with complex situations? When you're facing a problem you haven't encountered before, where the answers aren't clear, do you have the capacity to handle it by adapting and experimenting?	**p69**
	This practice will help you to grow that capacity.	
Know your stress language	Are you stressed? No, let's ask another question—do you know when you're stressed?	**p81**
	If you find this question surprising, this could be a great practice for you to try.	
Honour needs, not norms	Is everybody on your team able to make work work for them and perform at their best?	**p89**
	If not, it might be worth taking a close look at their individual needs.	
Manage your state	Are you having trouble connecting with your people? Do you find it difficult to inspire them at crucial times?	**p97**
	This practice will help you get your state in sync with theirs, which may be just what you need.	

Part 2—Team practices

Team tetris	Do some of your team have nothing to do while others are slammed? Are some bored and others stimulated?	p113
	This practice will help you balance that load to create efficiency and satisfaction in equal measure that lifts the whole team's wellbeing.	
Meeting makeovers	Are the meetings in your workplace creating brain-dead zombies instead of engaged, energised employees?	p123
	A meeting makeover may be the antidote.	
Quick, quality chats	Do you find it hard to connect with your team members because you don't have the time to get into a D&M with them? Or because you never talk except on Zoom?	p131
	This practice will show you how to create quality connections with your team in a matter of moments.	
Give (good) feedback; get (good) feedback	Do you know you should be giving your team feedback, but are afraid to do it? Or don't know how to do it? Or are you doing it only to find it backfires on you?	p141
	This practice will show you how to give and get feedback that grows you and your team.	
Learn together; grow together	Is your team the envy of the organisation? Does everybody want to join it? No?	p151
	This practice will help you create an amazing team that everyone wants to be on.	
Notice the need; find the noise	Do you find you're constantly putting out fires, only to have them re-ignite the second you turn your back? Are you wondering what you're doing wrong?	p159
	This practice will help you get to the root cause and extinguish those fires for good.	
Aligned purpose	Are you all on the same page and rowing in the same direction? Or is there discord and chaos that you can't find a cause for?	p169
	Aligning your purpose may be just what the doctor ordered.	
Great relationships	Is everybody in your organisation getting along like a house on fire? Or is your workplace more like a dysfunctional family living in a house that's burning down?	p177
	This practice will help you find harmony.	
Clear roles	Are you and your team members clear about what their role is? Are you all sticking to that role and running in the right lane? Or do you seem to be doing each other's work?	p185
	This practice will ensure everyone sticks to their own aisle and performance is enhanced.	

Part 3—Organisation practices

Built-in wellbeing	Is working for your organisation a health hazard? Or does your company provide a haven for workers?	**p201**
Human-centric change	Is an avalanche of change raining down on your organisation and causing everyone to lose their footing? If so, you need to think about not what is changing, but how you're changing. This practice will help you do that.	**p209**
Powerful engagement	Is your team engaged, excited and egging each other on to do better and better? No? Engagement is often misunderstood, but this practice will reveal the secrets to creating authentic engagement.	**p217**
Look before you leap	Are your innovation and change efforts backfiring? You may need guidance on how to anticipate and avoid unintended, unwelcome consequences.	**p227**
Constant curiosity	Is your organisation growing effortlessly? Is the table piled high with new ideas? Or is it stagnating? This practice will show you how to unleash childlike curiosity to turbocharge growth.	**p237**
Guided growth	Can your people see other people's perspectives? Are there a variety of viewpoints in the mix? This practice will ensure that everyone's opinion is sought and honoured, leading to more and different perspectives that grow the whole organisation.	**p245**
Take off and transform	Is your organisation missing out on opportunities? Struggling to stay ahead of the curve? Assessing your agility ability through this practice may be the antidote.	**p261**
Cultivate your culture	Is your organisation the envy of others? Are quality people hammering at the doors to get in? If that sounds desirable, this practice may help you boost your popularity.	**p275**
Mine some metaphors	Do you want to take your organisation to the next level? Do you want to learn a practice that nobody else is using? This one's for you.	**p283**

PART 1

INDIVIDUAL PRACTICES

WELCOME TO PART 1: Your Individual Practices. Here you'll find nine practices to support performance, growth and wellbeing at an individual level for both you and the people you lead.

Whether you lead yourself as an individual contributor, whether you're a newish leader or a senior leader, this is a great place to start. I've designed these practices in response to the real experiences of people just like you. I've interviewed them, I've heard about their challenges and frustrations, and I've designed this based on those insights.

Starting with yourself means starting with something small, something you can control more easily, something you can begin to build on. There is a gap between knowing and doing, and I've designed this section so you can close that gap to create change for yourself. It's about you, the person reading this book, deciding to learn new skills, change your habits, or improve how you work.

The practices in this section roughly equate to the one-day workshops and masterclasses I run with leaders, teams and organisations. These are designed to create immediate and noticeable change, get you energised, provide some quick wins for urgent relief and spark improvement.

While these practices are mostly directed at you, the leader, they can also help build the performance, growth and wellbeing of the individuals in your team so that everyone can feel good, do great and get better. After you've read and made some of these practices work for you, you can introduce them to others. As a leader, whether you're leading yourself, a team or many teams of people, I encourage you to start using the language and introducing these concepts to the people around you. Share a copy of this book with them and go through it together.

Are you ready to turbocharge your performance, spark growth and improve your wellbeing? And do you want to help the people around you experience those same improvements? Then turn the page and read on.

INDIVIDUAL
WELLBEING

WORK/LIFE CONTAMINATION

Barriers prevent contamination: clear barriers prevent work from poisoning your personal life.

IT'S 6:00 pm when you finally put your key in the front door. On the other side of that wooden barrier is home. The warm and familiar chaos of family life, with hugs, laughs and dinner around the table together. Or maybe your front door gives way to a solo space where you can curl up on the sofa for a blissful night of me-time and movies. Perhaps it's a much-anticipated date night for you and your partner. Whatever is on the other side of that door, it's your life—not your work. You pass the threshold, and... your phone pings. It's an urgent message from the office. You have to answer. Or maybe you have to cut your Netflix binge short because you're anxious about tomorrow's presentation and feel compelled to review your speaker notes. There might be a Zoom call scheduled for 10:00 pm because the client is on the other side of the world. Maybe when you walk through the door you're still in manager mode and find yourself ordering your partner around instead of offering to peel the potatoes or pick up the kids from footy practice. Or perhaps you're on autopilot while you say hi to the family; you pretend to listen, but your brain cannot switch off from the workday. It's happened again—your work has contaminated your life. You can almost hear the alarm going off: 'CODE RED! CODE RED! CONTAMINATION ALERT!'

When work contaminates our home life, it creates an infection that can damage our relationships and our health and rob our lives of meaning. In Australia, thirteen per cent of employees work very long hours—that's above the OECD average of ten percent. Australians also devote fewer hours in their day to personal care activities like eating and sleeping and leisure activities such as socialising and pursuing hobbies.[1]

We can try to fight it, but time and energy are finite resources. A feeling of helplessness sets in as we watch the contamination spread. Conflict—even all-out war—erupts between the different facets of our lives. When home life is going badly, we may try to compensate by working harder, which exacerbates the problem and plunges us into a vicious cycle. Our partner may find themselves picking up

---

[1] https://www.oecdbetterlifeindex.org/topics/work-life-balance/

the slack at home and having to sacrifice their own career, perpetuating that cycle.

The hybrid working model has opened the door for more contamination. An executive I work with now works from home three days a week. His kids love it—Dad can do more activities with them, but for him, it's a nightmare to juggle the logistics of footy, taekwondo, gymnastics and swimming. Compared to other roles, work is particularly intrusive, and the kids find themselves wishing Dad was smiling and watching their freestyle strokes instead of pacing by the side of the pool with a frown on his face and a phone glued to his ear. A longitudinal study conducted on how hybrid work is affecting working parents in Australia indicated that sixty-three per cent of employees experience issues managing work and family commitments, including unsocial and irregular hours and accommodating family demands.[2]

I'm certain you've heard of the problems with 'work/life balance'. In my coaching practice, it's one of the most common complaints I hear about from clients. The image that usually comes to mind is a pair of scales or a rusty old seesaw at the local park that produces an ear-piercing, discordant squeak with every movement. The word balance assumes we're weighing one thing against the other. That one wins, and one loses. That it's about sacrifice.

---

2   Laß, I., & Wooden, M. (2023). Working from Home and Work–Family Conflict. Work, Employment and Society, 37(1), 176-195. https://doi.org/10.1177/09500170221082474

This or that—work or family—career or fun. And it's a bit of a narrow view. Isn't work part of life? Who says work can be weighed against all the other aspects of life? Because it's not a matter of work OR life. It's work AND life. I want to call out this idea of 'balance' for the euphemism it is. I mean, when you're having a lot of fun in life and not working so much, you don't say you *lack* work/life balance, do you? You don't complain about a lack of 'boredom/ fun balance'. My clients have never complained about that! When I hear people say they don't have a work/life balance, ninety-nine per cent of the time, what they mean is they're working too much. And that work is spilling into their home life and spreading its contamination.

Research carried out in 2019 found that sixty-six per cent of employees had to work at night and were working more than ten hours a day. Sixty-seven per cent were reporting poor health caused by inadequate rest, and seventy per cent were working on Sundays to manage competing work and personal commitments.[3] Now, don't get me wrong—your long hours and weekend work might be working for you. If you're a swim coach, taking the kids to swimming lessons is no drama because you're at the pool all day anyway. Sometimes work and personal life can be combined successfully and even enhance each

---

3   Palumbo, R. (2020). Let me go to the office! an investigation into the side effects of working from home on work-life balance. [Side effects of working from home] *The International Journal of Public Sector Management, 33*(6), 771-790. doi:https://doi.org/10.1108/IJPSM-06-2020-0150

other. (See *Work/Life Wealth* for more on this.) What I'm talking about here is when work *interferes* with your personal life.

I get that many of us are living busy lives and that work can be competitive and pressured. Sometimes we have to take work home with us. Sometimes work and life must be traded against each other. These issues aren't going away, but we can strive for harmony over time, and this is what I work on with clients who complain about work/life balance.

Making it work

Consider for a moment, what do condoms, face masks and Sudocrem have in common? They're barriers: one is a barrier to sperm, one is a barrier to germs, and one creates a moisture barrier to prevent nappy rash. When it comes to preventing work/life contamination, you need to create barriers. There are three types of barriers we need to consider.

1 **Time**: when work is done and for how long. For example, I am open to working 9:00 am to 4:00 pm and 7.00 pm to 10:00 pm during the week, and on weekends I'm open to working for up to five hours. I call this the **Day Divide**.

2 **Place**: where work is done and not done. For example, I am open to working in my home office, at co-working spaces and onsite with clients. I am not open to working at the gym or in my bedroom. I call this **Location Lock**.

3   **Personal**: what your limits are, where you've set them, what you're willing to tolerate and not tolerate, and what you say no to. For example, a pregnant woman may need to set a boundary around having her belly touched or listening to horror birth stories. I think of this as the **Safety Circle**.

To create barriers, you need to get clear on where you are now. If you want to change and get somewhere else, you won't know the way unless you know your starting point. To figure out where you are, I'd like to introduce you to what I call the Work/life Contamination Code. This code is inspired by the emergency codes in hospitals, such as 'Code Blue', which means a patient needs immediate medical attention, or 'Code Black', which means there's a bomb somewhere. Yikes! If you're a parent, you might be familiar with 'Code Brown', which indicates

Code	Incident Definition
Code Red	Trouble at home means you're making up for it and **compensating** at work, or vice versa.
Code Yellow	Mission out. You're **sacrificing** home life due to demands at work, or vice versa.
Code Brown	Hazardous spill due to flimsy barriers.
All Clear	Clear, firm barriers. Work and life are not in conflict.

FIGURE 2 Work/life Contamination Code

that a child has deposited a contaminant in the swimming pool. Ugh.

You can use the code to raise awareness about what's going on with you, determine which 'alert level' you're at and whether you need to take action to reduce work/life contamination. The goal is to avoid getting to the stage where the alarm starts screeching, 'CODE RED!' or 'CODE YELLOW!' or 'CODE BROWN!'

To find out your current alert level, answer these questions. Remember that the examples given are just examples—what's appropriate for one person may not be appropriate for you.

Q. How firm is your **Day Divide**?

- Do you have rules about when you work that work for your specific needs and personal situation? (E.g., not working on weekends or not working after 6:00 pm.)

- Are you following these rules?

Q. How firm is your **Location Lock**?

- Do you have rules about where you work that work for your specific needs and personal situation? (E.g. not working in your bedroom or in the garden.)

- Are you following these rules?

Q. How firm is your **Safety Circle**?

- Do you have rules about protecting your body and mind that work for your specific needs and personal situation? (E.g. not hugging or kissing people 'hello' who you don't know well.)

- Are you following these rules?

If you answered 'yes' to these questions, you're in the 'All Clear' zone. Firm barriers provide good protection against contamination. If you answered 'no' to any of them, your alert level is Code Brown, and you are probably experiencing work/life contamination.

Now, let's ask some more questions to assess the nature of the contamination.

Q. Are you **sacrificing**? For example:

- Have you sacrificed family time or frequently skipped activities that are valuable to you personally because you need to show up and be on site at work?

- Are you underperforming at work because family time is intruding into your working hours?

If you answered 'yes' to either of these questions, your alert level is Code Yellow. Sacrifice can make us resent our work, which can lead to chronic stress. Action is required to create firmer barriers.

Q. Are you **compensating**? For example:

- Do you throw yourself into work to compensate for things not going well at home?

- Are you looking for positive experiences at home to compensate for negative work experiences?

If you answered 'yes' to either of these questions, your alert level is Code Red. When we compensate, we fail to address the root cause of a problem. Action is required to create firmer barriers.

It's important to create barriers for the sake of your wellbeing, but you also need to share them. Draw on your relationships for support and accountability. Finding the right words for this is important, and it's something my coaching clients have found valuable. What we say matters, whether we're talking to ourselves in our heads or out loud with our friends or workmates. Next time you want to say you have no work/life balance, try being more specific. Tell it how it is. Because when you do this, you can do something about it. As Dr Daniel J. Siegel, professor of psychiatry, says, 'Name it to tame it.' I have always believed that sunlight really is the best disinfectant.

So don't just say, 'I want work-life balance.' Try saying something like:

- I've got work-life **contamination** because ...

- At work, I'm **making up** for ...

- At home, my work stress is **spilling** onto my family...

- I'm **sacrificing** my social life to get that project over the line and score that promotion...

- I've **prioritised** x to protect my wellbeing...

The poet Robert Frost said, 'Fences make good neighbours.' Sometimes, elements of your personal and working life can support each other, but if they clash, it's important to segment your life and keep the barrier between work and non-work quite distinct. Sacrificing, compensating and failing to keep your barriers clear will not work in the long run. Time and energy aren't renewable resources, so use the work/life code regularly to check your barriers and make adjustments if necessary. I want you to go to work and feel good, and I also know that your alert level will change over time, so I recommend revisiting these questions regularly.

When it comes to barriers, there's no set-and-forget. Just like driving a car, sometimes you need the brake, and sometimes you need the accelerator. If you want to make work work for you and strive towards excellence in your leadership, you need to be aware of when to give that wellbeing pedal an extra push. And you may find that when your wellbeing improves, so does your growth and performance. Everything is connected.

WORK/LIFE
WHIPLASH

Stop the snap: DEFEND yourself from the strain of switching between work and life.

WHEN AN out-of-control car slams into a telephone pole, the driver's head is snapped violently backwards. Then, at the mercy of momentum, their head snaps violently towards the steering wheel. Then it snaps backwards again. SNAP! SNAP! SNAP! Whiplash is a serious injury that can cause lifelong issues with pain and restricted movement. And the individual has no control over it—they're victims of circumstance.

Now, imagine you have to design a work strategy that affects multiple stakeholders and requires sifting through mountains of information. Your desk is in a busy open-plan office, where it's difficult to concentrate deeply, so you get up super early one morning and set up your laptop on the dining room table. In the quiet of the early morning, the creative, effective solution you need starts to emerge, then— SNAP! A tearful toddler flings the door open, complaining of a nightmare. You tuck the tot back into bed and turn back to your computer. But the spell has been broken, and the clever concept you were shaping in your mind has dissolved. Later that day at the office, you're lucky enough to find an empty meeting room where you can work on your strategy in peace. You spend some time getting back into the groove, then—SNAP! A pop-up appears on your screen, reminding you that the plumber is coming tomorrow and you have to call to confirm the details. You call, leave a message, and then once again turn back to your important work. The solution starts to take shape again, then SNAP! Your phone rings. It's the plumber. You could ignore the call, but the second it rang, your concentration was broken. You sigh, swipe to answer, and anticipate another late night at the office.

The term I've coined to describe this phenomenon is 'work/life whiplash', which is what happens when work and home life collide. As you switch between work/home/leader/dad, you find your head flicking every which way and doing untold damage. The rise of hybrid working has both highlighted and embedded this problem. Adding to the damage is work-work whiplash. This happens when you're forced to switch rapidly from one task or area of focus to another, and the loss of concentration damages productivity. It's been discovered that employees nowadays switch tasks every three minutes and fifteen seconds and switch contexts every ten minutes and thirty seconds.[4]

Whiplash—whether it's work whiplash, work-life whiplash or both—is a serious problem. We lose time, momentum, productivity and energy. The modern trope of the competent multitasker, powering through their workday with a phone in one hand and a sushi roll in the other while their toes type away on the laptop at their elbow, is not much better than a myth. While there are some neuro-types who can multi-task, the majority of people can't. It might feel like we're getting a lot done when we're doing a lot of things at once, but research has revealed this to be largely wishful thinking.

Work whiplash has been found to reduce productivity by eighty-three per cent, with employees experiencing issues such as limited task focus and underperformance.[5] Forty-five per cent of people say context-switching makes them less productive, and forty-three per cent say switching between tasks causes fatigue.[6] It's also been found that task switching prevents you from achieving the flow

---

4   The claim that employees switch tasks every three minutes and fifteen seconds and switch contexts every ten minutes and thirty seconds appears to originate from research by Gloria Mark, a professor at the University of California, Irvine, through studies conducted over several years.

5   Xu, Shan, Kerk Kee, and Chang Mao. Multitasking and Work-Life Balance: Explicating Multitasking When Working from Home. *Journal of Broadcasting & Electronic Media* 65, no. 3 (2021): 397–425. doi:10.108%0883815I.2021.1976 779

6   https://www.atlassian.com/blog/productivity/context-switching

state that supports deep work and that concentration cannot be easily regained—it takes time. Whiplash damages many areas of our working lives, and buried under this pile of rubble is our wellbeing

When work/life whiplash is layered on top of work/work whiplash, it adds complexity as both task and role are switched simultaneously. The growing variety of tech that litter our lives and that we need for our jobs has added yet another layer of complexity as we switch from app to app and device to device. Research has revealed that people are switching between fifteen different types of tech every day. That is crazy.

Whiplash is everywhere, and when so many aspects of our working lives are compromised, the collateral damage is a loss of personal wellbeing.

Making it work

So, what do we do? Barricade our office door? Not quite, although safety measures do form part of the solution. In fact, in an ideal world we would put safety measures in place that prevent whiplash from occurring. But no safety measures are foolproof, so dealing with whiplash when it happens also forms part of the mitigating strategy.

Introducing the 3 Ds Tool, a simple framework I've developed to help you deal with competing demands in life and work.

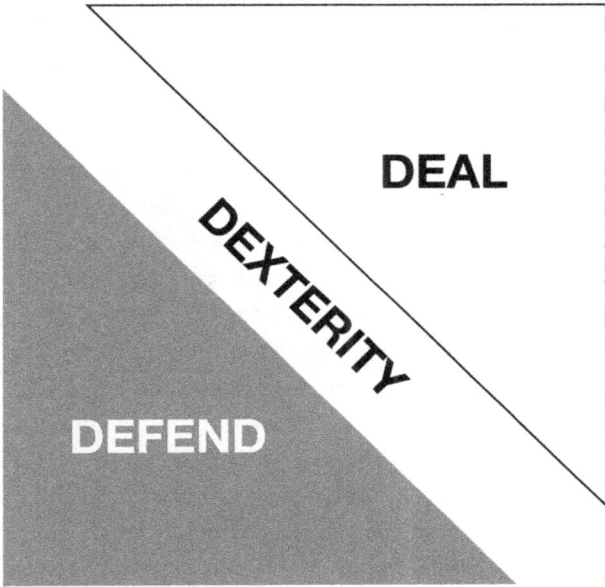

FIGURE 3 The 3 Ds

The first D in this model is **defend**, and as the word suggests, it's your first defence against work/life and work/work whiplash. This is about proactively scheduling your time, consciously choosing where you work and setting up your environment to minimise the risk of 'injury'. For example, if you don't want to be interrupted, put a 'do not disturb' sign on your office door before you plunge into deep work—don't wait for that first interruption before taking this step. If you think your clever signage will be ignored, physically remove yourself to another location to complete your deep work for the day. If you're expecting a call from the plumber, try calling them first and sorting things out so you're not interrupted. Or mute your notifications. Better yet, just turn your phone off.

There have been many trends in workflow management, time management and productivity. I'm sure some of it is useful, but I know from working with my clients that everyone is unique, and our needs are always changing based on many factors. So take some time to look at your personal situation and design measures to protect yourself from whiplash. You may need to experiment with different practices to see what works for you. Some of you may find that safety measures are difficult to put in place in your situation, but we can at least be aware of the real risk of whiplash. Where your awareness goes, your energy flows. Just being mindful of this risk will be helpful.

Of course, not even the best plans are foolproof, which is where the second D, **dexterity**, comes in. You need to plan for the unexpected. You need to be ready for that moment when your carefully designed safety measures break down, and you need to regroup. You need to accept that sometimes this will happen. That it's inevitable. Knowing this and being prepared will help you find the dexterity to pivot and deal with the interruptions. This brings us to the third D.

The third D is to **deal** with the whiplash. At some point, we're all going to be interrupted and forced to switch gears, no matter how many safety measures we put in place. In my case, I often have to flick the switch to go quickly from leader to attentive mum. In a work situation, you might go straight from a brutal meeting to holding space in a one-on-one with your direct report. When this happens, you need to put your hand on that gear stick and make a shift. If you don't, you'll be over-revving your engine, screeching towards a brick wall and putting yourself at risk of whiplash.

What you need are transition tactics to help you get those revs under control in the heat of the moment. As a pianist, this quote from Mozart has always resonated with me: 'The music is not in the notes but in the silence between.' The space between the notes is where the music comes alive. This is what transition tactics are.

Transition tactics based on mindfulness skills are helpful. These skills help ground you and boost awareness of where you're at and how you're feeling so you can focus on what's in front of you. It's also important to know that not every type of mindfulness activity works for everyone. There is no right way. You have to find the right 'way in' for you. So below, I've included a few transition tactics that suit different types of brains—a.k.a. neurotypes.

The 'comma'

What is a comma anyway? It's a short punctuation mark that indicates you need to take a pause.

This exercise is about wiping the slate clean and creating a bit of space before you go from one thing to the other. There are four steps:

1 Balance your body; be upright. If you're sitting, pop your feet on the ground.

2 Relax your body by taking one or two deep breaths and consciously release the tension on your exhale.

3 Let your breath settle and your attention rest.

4 Tune in to your environment and sounds.

That's it. Why not try it right now?

The '5,4,3,2,1'

I like this technique because it uses our senses, which are powerful tools that can quickly ground us in the present if we only have a moment. I find this activity particularly powerful with clients who need to stop their thoughts from spinning but for whom breathing or visualising techniques aren't right. It goes like this:

• What are five things you can **see**? Look around and notice five things you haven't seen before. Maybe a pattern on a wall, rays of light shining through a window, or the facial expressions of people nearby.

• What are four things you can **feel**? Maybe you can feel your jaw clenching or the space between your eyes tightening, your hair resting on your shoulders or a breeze on your skin. Try picking up an object and notice its texture and weight.

- What are three things you can **hear**? Notice all the background sounds of your environment. Can you hear people typing? Is there music, or what does the silence itself sound like?

- What are two things you can **smell**? Take a slow, deep breath in. Maybe you can smell coffee brewing, a neighbour's perfume, or food in the microwave. It doesn't have to be a nice smell; maybe there's a trash can nearby or the air is stagnant and still.

- What is one thing you can **taste**? Move your tongue around in your mouth. Simply notice how your mouth tastes. Or try taking a bite of chocolate or popping a piece of gum in your mouth. You can also 'taste' the air to see how it feels on your tongue.

Do you notice any difference in your state of mind now? Are you less caught up in the emotional storm (or 'difficult' thoughts and feelings)? Is it easier for you to be present and focus? Has that engine stopped revving?

мс Hammer

If the previous techniques don't appeal or aren't effective, perhaps a mantra could work for you. Something along the lines of 'Stop, hammer time!'

can give you a bit of a jolt and help bookend what you're doing so you can move on to the next thing with a bit of intention and presence. For me, music is a powerful way to shift my state and focus. It moves my attention from what I'm doing and how I'm feeling to something outside myself. Working from home, some days I don't have time to pop on a tune before taking ten steps out of my office and into the living room where I switch into mum mode. Using a song lyric as a mantra and busting the smallest move helps me make the switch and avoid whiplash. I think about MC Hammer's 80s dance moves.

Interruptions to our workflow—from both work itself and our personal lives—are inevitable. In fact, work whiplash is on the increase. And it can undermine excellence. If whiplash is a problem for you, lean into the three Ds model. These simple exercises may be just what you need to manage transitions more smoothly, give that wellbeing pedal a quick push, and get work working for you again.

WORK/LIFE
WEALTH

Create your own work/life wealth:
Let different parts of your life boost
each other so you can live your best life.

I WAS WORKING with a senior leader who was up
against multiple challenges—leading organisational
transformations and restructuring, supporting his
partner in a career change, and dealing with his kid's
issues. His regular exercise routine had crashed and
burned, and he was back to having lunch at his desk if
he had lunch at all. He joked about his 'dad bod', but
I could hear the serious undertone. So, I suggested
that we go for a walk for our next coaching session. He
chose the spot, and we met at the beach, finishing
our session with a takeaway coffee. This idea was so
successful it became the ritual for our coaching sessions. He'd choose an outdoor location, text me ahead
of time so I knew what shoes to wear, and we'd hike
and coach, beach and coach, or coffee and coach.

This became our coaching ritual because meeting outdoors and occasionally enjoying a local coffee gave both of us a generous helping of what I have dubbed 'work/life wealth'. My client was able to get the exercise and fresh air he'd been missing during working hours without blocking out extra time in his day. I also enjoyed being outdoors and away from my desk. Buying our coffee at the local café supported the community and helped us feel connected to it. What my client got through these sessions was a much-needed dose of work/life wealth. I came up with this term to describe what happens when different parts of your life boost each other instead of competing.

We all know that a busy life, with all its demands and responsibilities, can be stressful. Sometimes, you have to create barriers to keep different areas of your life separate, but there is an alternative. A busy, demanding life can be enriching; if handled right, it creates a kind of wealth. A rich life means having a full life and playing in different areas: work, home, family, community, friends and yourself. Living a synergistic life—where everything aligns and flows together—makes everything easier and more enjoyable. The wealth comes from wise investing. When you don't put all your eggs in one basket but diversify your 'investments', you get a more steady and reliable return. And the dividends you get can be re-invested in areas where you're trying to build something meaningful.

I believe you can be successful in work, not *despite* your home life, but *because* of it. When my business received funding from the Australian Government to support workplace engagement and participation, we created the World of Work Program. Through this, we supported 500 women in re-entering the workforce or changing careers. I will never forget one woman I coached who'd been a mid-level manager before deciding to stop work and be at home full time. She said to me, 'I've been at home looking after kids for years; what do you want me to put on my resume? That I can multi-task doing the laundry and making endless snacks?' She was kidding, of course, but of the many things I coached her through, the standout quality was her level of distress tolerance. She had mastered the skill of managing moments of complete overwhelm. It was incredible. She developed this skill to cope with the many stresses going on in her family life, which included having a disabled child. Through necessity, she had created a range of tools to man-age moments of intense stress and regulate her emotions. Emotions are contagious. You never give a crying baby to a crying adult, right? Through her mastery of this skill, my client was regulating her whole family—not just the kids but also her hus-band, who often came home from work stressed.

Being able to regulate the emotions of the peo-ple around you is an invaluable skill for leaders. It was my client's difficult home life that gifted her this skill, a skill she could offer to potential employees as she re-entered the workforce. This is an example of work and home life coming together and creating an additional edge for you as you move towards excellence. And it's not an unusual story. The key is to try to recognise these windows of opportunity—places where one area of your life can support and enhance another.

It's a win-win.

Actually, it's more than a win-win. It can be a win-win-win. Or even a win-win-win-win. The concept of the four-way win was developed by Stewart D. Friedman. A four-way win is that sweet spot where home life, work, community and self come together. It's about making intelligent choices about how you use your time and attention so you're not having to make a trade-off. All you need are small changes. Walking and talking outdoors during coaching sessions with my client is a perfect example. He was working on his professional development through our coaching session while reaping from the therapeutic effects of nature. I was in my work role while experiencing those same therapeutic effects. By visiting our local café, we contributed to the wealth of the community. And because we both went home in a good mood after a fulfilling day at work, our families benefitted as well.

Making it work

Creating work/life wealth is about looking at where different areas of your life overlap and provide a window of opportunity for an 'investment'. I came up with the model for this idea when I was staring meditatively (is that a word?) at the leadlight window in the front door of my house. You may have seen these windows with coloured glass panels that (appear to) overlap and create new colours.

The model on the next page builds on the work of Stewart Friedman and expands the four-way win to a five-way window. I've found that this enables people to think more deeply, broadly and specifically about pinpointing where to build energy, creativity, and so on—that is, their 'wealth'. The five-way window provides a scaffolding of sorts that helps make this exercise practical.

As you can see, each circle represents one area of life: home and family, community, work, self (me) and friends. To create work/life wealth, the trick is to look for activities that can dwell in more than one circle. In other words, activities that take place where the circles overlap. As you can see from the model, when you do this, it can boost your energy and health, satisfy your creative urge, improve your focus and productivity, enhance your wellbeing and create a sense of meaning in your life.

Let me give you an example from my own life. You may be surprised to know that I'm a qualified make-up artist. It began as a hobby and blossomed

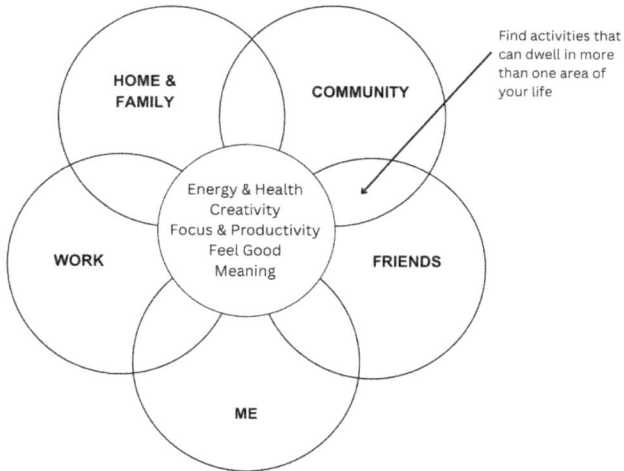

FIGURE 4 The 5-way Window

into a truly enriching aspect of my life that sits at the point where all five key areas meet. It's something I can do for myself that helps me feel good and taps into my creativity. It deepens my connection with friends because I can do their make-up on important occasions, and we enjoy that bonding time. I also volunteer to do the make-up for girls in foster homes before they go to their school formals. That's a way that I can give back to the community and give my life meaning. It's also a peaceful, calming kind of activity with a sensory focus, which helps both myself and my neurodivergent daughter reset our nervous systems. That enriches my home life and enhances my focus and productivity. The benefits to my professional life are more obvious. I can do my own make-up for on-camera work, and I'm able to give valuable make-up tips to my clients to enhance their professionalism and presentation.

Now it's your turn. Get out a sheet of paper and draw up the five-way window as shown in the model. Have a think about activities that take place where the different areas cross each other and overlap. Those are your windows of opportunity. Now, I don't want you to feel pressured to find activities that involve all five areas. For heaven's sake, don't think that you can only take up hobbies that are in service to your work. It's totally fine to do an activity just because you like it. But if you can find activities in the areas that overlap, your life will be richer. So be on the lookout. Sniff out opportunities to create work/life wealth. Some will be successful. Others will not. And that's good because you've tried them, and now you can move forward.

As you keep looking for ways to create work/life wealth, you'll notice that the different parts of your life stop clashing so much. It's less about choosing one over the other and more about making everything work together in harmony. I believe you can be successful at work, not despite your personal life, but because of it. When your work and personal life support each other, it gives you an extra edge as a leader moving towards excellence.

INDIVIDUAL GROWTH

BUILD CHANGE-MAKING ENERGY

Build energy to change and grow: Know your reasons and make change easier.

LET'S TALK about change. You might not want to, but we have to. Because the fact is, change is everywhere. Apart from death and taxes, change is the only certainty in life. Sometimes it's something you *want* to do, like becoming more present at home in your significant relationship. Sometimes it's something you *have* to do, such as cutting out fried foods after a heart attack. That's what happened to my dad. Change can be something you *do to yourself*, like changing career tracks or trying your hand at being self-employed and joining the gig economy. Change can also be something *done to you*, such as your role being made redundant through a restructure. Or, indeed, being given greater responsibilities after a restructure.

And no doubt you've heard all the clichés...change is hard...people don't like change...we're not good at change. Clichés often earn their status because they're true (that in itself is a cliché)—but not these ones: at best, they're myths; at worst, excuses. When we're asked the question, 'Who wants change?' we all put our hands up! We can see the benefits and intellectually understand why the change is required, but many change efforts fail. It's rarely painless, and it requires energy. Many leaders and teams I work with are struggling to reap the benefits of growth from it.

Change can be painful. That much is true. When my husband was a child, around ten years old the story goes, he cried every night from physical growing pains, and his mum had to rub goanna oil into his legs. Yes, it can be uncomfortable, and even the change that you want to make can be hard, painful, confronting and draining.

Neuroscience tells us that resisting change isn't something we consciously do. Rather, we resist change instinctively because we're hard-wired to protect ourselves and our current state, which helps us survive—our brains have an inherent need for stability. It's normal to feel anxious and show resistance in the face of change. Now, I want to add that this isn't true for everyone. For example, some ADHDers, myself included, have a neurotype that *craves* novelty, newness and change. But if you *are* the type of person who resists change, I have good news: neuroscience also tells us that we can grow our capacity to change. To do that, however, we need more than goanna oil.

I invite you to look at change in a new way. To go wider and deeper. The key is understanding that it's not the change itself that's tough. Change can be incredibly rewarding. What really stings is the steps to get there, like getting on that treadmill for the first time after your doctor warns you about your health or making that phone call to a recruitment firm after the restructure. That's the hard part.

Whatever type of change you're undergoing—voluntary or involuntary, positive or negative—one thing is true. Change is your ticket to growth. Growth happens through change. There is no other way. There's no shortcut or cheat sheet or magic potion. If you wish to grow as a leader—or grow in any way as a person—you must master your moves as you step towards change. Like anything, you must be intentional about this. Leadership is a behaviour, not a position. We all have to lead ourselves through change.

Regardless of the type of change looming on your horizon, there are tools to help you find the energy needed to get started and get through those tricky transition points. That energy is your ignition source. It's like the fierce growl a Formula 1 car makes as the engine roars into life and escalates to a high-pitched scream that reverberates through the air. It's electrifying. Even the spectators can feel the fierce, raw energy as the car fights to be set free. Once you have that initial boost of energy, provided you have enough fuel in the tank to get you around the track again and again, you'll achieve the change you desire.

Let me unpack this a bit more by telling you about my friend Denzil, who achieved significant change in his life and generously shared his reflections with me in the hope they would help others.

Denzil, or 'Denz' as we like to call him, was an engineer—both in work and in life. Apart from playing golf once a week, he'd never been very athletic, and he loved the beers after work. By the time he hit his mid-thirties, Denz was focused on his kids and work, not himself, and was putting on some serious weight (his words, not mine). I'm sure a lot of us can relate. The first hint that he should make a change in his life came on a holiday in Noosa. He was out paddleboarding with a friend the same age, who flew across the water effortlessly and left a red-faced Denzil panting in his wake. Obviously, he needed to do something about his fitness.

Like I said, Denz is an engineer, and his engineering brain looked at the situation from a technical point of view. He thought about efficiency and noted that fit people run efficiently. Sounds good. So he bought himself some running shoes and headed down to the local oval. Again, being an engineer, he broke this 'running' caper down to its essential parts and then built it back up. First, he'd run about a hundred metres, then walk a hundred metres. He did about six laps like this. After a while, he was able to run further; before long, he could do multiple laps. And before you could say 'heart attack,' Denz had joined a local running group, made friends in the running community, logged on to Strava and signed up for running events. He's now collecting medals left, right and centre.

What's really fascinating is that now, if Denzil doesn't run, he experiences an uncomfortable build-up of energy. Running releases that energy and takes him to a calm space from where he can deal with the issues that life throws at him—work, kids, relationships. At the time of writing, Denz was running 20-40 km a week without fail. He's even integrated this into how he spends time with his kids, who are cheering him on at events and riding their bikes alongside him as he trains.

'Running is my weapon,' he once said to me with a laugh.

You can see, from Denzil's story, that the key is to get your engine roaring into life—like that F1 car. You have to ignite the flame. Denzil was able to do this successfully because he broke his goal down into smaller milestones and focused on working towards the next one rather than trying to change everything at once. With that flame burning, motivation begins to spread like wildfire. When the transition point has been passed, that change you wanted to make, or had to make, or had done to you stops feeling painful and becomes energising. When the fire is roaring within you, it ignites an inner drive to take action and achieve goals. And that motivation can be catching. Your flame will energise the people around you who will feel their own motivation surge.

If you want something different, you have to do or be something different. And this takes energy. So, let's build the energy you need to get started and keep going through the process of change.

Making it work

I'd like to introduce you to the Gearbox Boost. But first, I have to thank Dr Michael Cavanagh and Dr Travis Kemp for introducing me to the guts of this model, which is informed by the transtheoretical model of change. They have both been instrumental in my growth as an executive coach, and I can't thank Dr Trav enough for my growth as a human.[7]

This model is inspired by a manual car's four-on-the-floor gearbox. Just like a Formula 1 car, this tool will get you roaring out of the starting grid, keep your tyres gripping like glue as you speed around corners and ensure you stay on track for lasting change.

At first glance, this might look like a fancy version of a pros and cons list. But in my experience the pros and cons lists never work. For each point

---

7   Dr Michael Cavanagh is Deputy Director of the Coaching Psychology Unit at University of Sydney and Director of the Institute of Coaching and Consulting Psychology. Dr Travis Kemp is Co-director of the Institute of Coaching and Consulting Psychology, a coaching, consulting, business and performance psychologist, and investor advisor to start-ups and scale-ups.

you put down, you just end up writing the opposite of it on the other side of the list and pretty much end up with lots of dot points on both sides of the ledger, leading to more confusion. It doesn't help with making a decision to change, and the process of writing doesn't build fire in your belly. I want you to scrap that pros and cons list. Screw it up. Instead, get a piece of paper, fold it into four, and draw it up like the diagram below. As you can see, this exercise will clarify the upside and downside of changing, as well as the upside and downside of staying the same, which makes it a little bit different from a pros and cons list and a whole lot more powerful.

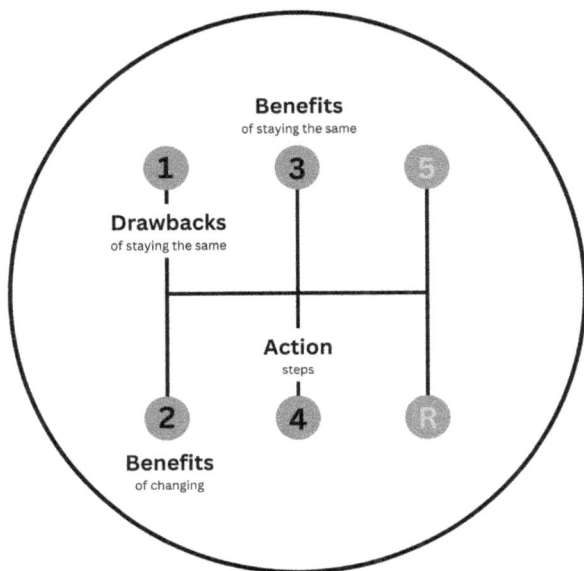

FIGURE 5 Gearbox Boost

I introduced this model to a leader in one of my programs, who really took to it and even applied it to his smoking habit. Here's how he filled it in.

First gear—The **drawbacks** of staying the same: health risks, smell and cost.

Second gear—The **benefits** of making the change: save money, be healthier, breathe better, live longer, see my children grow up, and maybe become a great-grandparent.

Third gear—The **benefits** of staying the same: gives me a break and helps me relax.

Fourth gear—The **action steps** needed to make the change happen: throw out all lighters, cigarette packets, ashtrays, go see a hypnotherapist, say I'm a non-smoker, say I'm going to breathe fresh air for the rest of my life.

This exercise is powerful because it taps into both sides of our brain—the left, with its focus on logic and language, and the right, with its focus on feeling, imagination and desire. In the example above, connecting the change to something bigger—in this case, living longer and becoming a great-grandparent—fulfils that function. By engaging the imagination and positive emotions, we create a new neural pathway. We engage the brain in your head and the brain in your heart. And when both your head and heart are engaged, you will find more energy to make that change.

The other factor that makes this exercise powerful is listing out the positives of *not* changing, which may seem counterintuitive. But by doing this, you acknowledge the payoff inherent in the behaviour, and you can see it for what it is. With that payoff acknowledged and out in the open, it's easier to let it go.

You can use the Gear Box Boost to build energy to change in almost any area of your life. It's quick and simple, and it also evolves—you can keep adding to the boxes. So I urge you to give it a try. Once you get a purchase on that change you want to make, you'll find the energy might be just the beginning of a whole revolution of personal growth. When you master the art of personal growth, you bring energy and expertise into your work place and begin to make work work for you and everybody around you. Change is inevitable in both our personal and working lives. Learn to embrace it, feel its power and let it drive you down the road to excellence.

DRIVE YOUR
DEVELOPMENT

Grow yourself, grow your organisation:
Create a growth plan that energises you
and aligns with your organisation's goals.

SO YOU KNOW how at festivals there's always something going on... You've usually got your main stage for the big acts and there are smaller stages with emerging artists performing. There are food trucks, and there might be an art installation. There are interactive activities that keep everybody entertained and engaged. It's a whirlwind of excitement and energy, and every time you turn a corner, you find something new to experience. The atmosphere is electric, and you're constantly discovering and engaging with all the different elements that make the festival unique.

Now imagine you're at a festival, and you feel drawn towards one particular tent for some reason.

Inside there's a woman dressed in purple festival gear and dripping with exotic jewellery. She presents you with a glass triangle and says, 'This is your triangle of choice.' You pick it up and look more closely. On one side of the triangle is the word 'Peak'; on another side is the word 'Plateau'; on the third side is the word 'Pull'. The triangle is asking you a question. Do you want to Peak? Plateau? Or Pull yourself and others down?

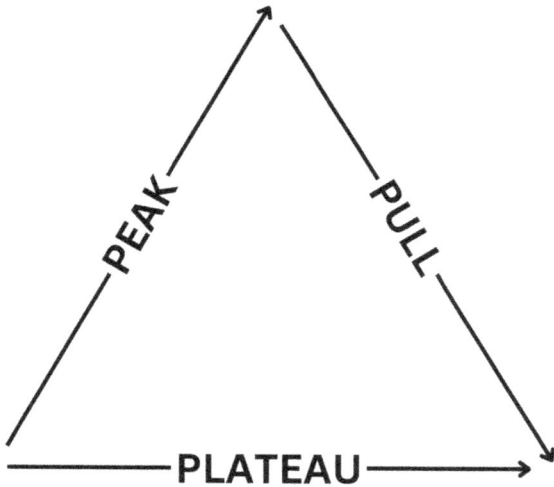

FIGURE 6 The Triangle of Choice

I'm no fortune teller, but I know what you'll pick. I know you want to peak. You want to grow and reach your potential. Development is important to you. You want to grow in your role. You want to build depth and breadth; and grow your scope and skillset. To peak, you need to have clear, focused efforts. You need action with intelligence. You can't just spin your wheels and hope your existing skills and capability will get you by. You need the intention. The focus.

I know that you want to peak, but meaningful, truly impactful development that grows you to the edge of your excellence is not always sought by leaders. Do you have the skills you need to keep you at the forefront of your profession? Can you not just fulfil but exceed the requirements of your role? If not, step up and do the training you need to give you that edge of excellence. I know you want to peak; training will help you do that. And if you want to peak, you will have to be prepared for your next role. Sure, you may not know what it will be but think about where you'd like to go next and plug any skill gaps you can identify. The wonderful thing about skills is that they're transferable. You can take that toolkit wherever you go; it adds to your versatility and employability.

Skills allow you to do your job, but they can also benefit you in unexpected ways, such as by revealing new ways to do things and identifying opportunities. Before I built my business, I had managed large budgets in senior roles. But I didn't know the basics, as I never had revenue targets or accountability for a P&L. When I started my business, I had to build my financial acumen skills deliberately and consciously. Not only did this help me make sense of my P&L, it helped me see growth opportunities that might otherwise have been hidden from view.

These days, training is easier to access. It's often available on the job and in smaller, bite-sized modules. It can be conducted both formally and informally and through many platforms, including structured courses, one-on-one coaching, mentoring and more. Microlearning is happening all the time, and the beauty of education through small doses is that it can be truly laser-focused and relevant.

Accessing learning is not a problem; the real question is—what should you learn? No one is interested in growth for growth's sake or learning for learning's sake. Unless you're a child, in which case every moment of every day is a glorious learning experience. As adults, the skills and capabilities we seek to learn must be relevant. The skill must fit the role. Otherwise, it's like trying to stick Lego and Duplo together.

A good development plan will give you focus so you can peak and reach your potential. It will help you to know what to focus on now and what can wait. Picture yourself at the bottom of the mountain, looking at that peak you aspire to. You could spread your efforts across ten tasks, stepping forward a little bit with each. Or you could concentrate on just one task, and with every focused step, you leap forward a good ten steps. If you chase two rabbits, you won't catch either of them. It's the same with development. If you split your focus across too many things, you won't achieve any of them. So, put a strategy in place. Decide what's in and what's out. Focusing on a few things will lead to greater progress.

When you look at a development plan, think about what's currently happening, what needs to happen, and what the gap is between those things—the skills that need to be built to move forward. Think about skills in terms of outcome—of the shifts you want to make.

Now let's take it further. Let's get to the heart of the matter. Where they exist, development plans are a tick-the-box. They're in the system, tick. Done. Everybody has one, so we can go home now. Not quite. I have yet to see an organisation where everyone not only has a development plan but has one that's energising for the person and aligned to the needs of the organisation.

Usually I see a list of tactics—of things a person is going to do—that's a mix of formal learning, reading, and perhaps some on-the-job learning. And there's nothing wrong with that, but we're still missing the gold. For a development plan to be energising for the person, we need to plug in to their values and strengths. It must include have-to goals but also love-to and want-to goals.

Your values are your compass in chaos, fuelling your drive and defining your why. Being clear on what you care about helps with direction and motivation. When we act in alignment with our values, we express our strengths, and when we leverage our strengths, we can better live out our values. This is important for growth, but also feeds into wellbeing and supports performance.

Connecting your development to your values and strengths fuels your enthusiasm. Scott Adams, the creator of the Dilbert comic strip, says that enthusiasm, conviction and belief are worth twenty-five IQ points. When you talk about your development—the goals and the things you're focusing on every day—I want to see you LIGHT up.

Love-to and want-to goals must be linked not just to the person's role but also to the *needs of the organisation*. This point is critical. You need a development plan that's fit for both the person and the purpose. You must ask yourself, 'What does the strategy of the organisation require of me?'

Let me tell you about Ali. He worked as an analyst in operations for a large organisation, but wanted to develop and become an accomplished project manager. Giving back and contributing to society were key values of his. The organisation's strategy had a big focus on transformation and was investing capital heavily into projects. To get some mentoring, coaching and experience in project management while he was in his ops role, Ali initiated a project to get a new boat for the kids in his home town in Africa so they could travel more safely to school. Ali and his team delivered that boat, and Ali went on to be a successful project manager and product owner. All three notes were hit—Ali underwent development, that development aligned with his values, and that development also supported the organisation's strategy.

Making it work

Let's put this into a practical, step-by-step process:

1 Think about a key value of yours.

2 Link that value to a growth goal—a want-to or love-to goal in this case.

3 Think about how this aligns with

- The strategy of the organisation

- Your current role

These first three steps are the ones that will transform your development plan from a tick-the-box to an energy source that will both benefit the organisation and supercharge your growth.

Now let's make an action plan to pursue this goal. Ask yourself:

4 How can you get some exposure to see what great looks like?

5 How might you get some hands-on experience to try for yourself?

6 Who or what is available in your community to help you learn and grow?

7 What new communities could you be part of?

8 Is coaching/mentoring suitable?

9 What formal learning is available?

10 Are there small experiments you might try?

Your development plan is important to both you and the overall organisation. When you find growth goals that are aligned with your values, you play to your strengths. When you have goals that don't just tick a box but light you up, everybody benefits. Work starts to work for you, and you are one step closer to excellence.

BUILD MINDSET X

Master Mindset X:
Leaders must build Mindset X to lead change
and drive growth through uncertainty.

DO YOU have the skills and energy to do your job? Yes? Good. And now I have another question for you... How full is your cup? Is there room for more? Can you power through the demands of your day and still have 'a little something' left over to draw on when a critical project goes pear-shaped at 5:00 pm on the Friday before a long weekend? Is there room in your cup to absorb more pressure? Or will it spill over? To be clear, I'm not talking about tea here. I'm talking about capacity. What is your capacity? Is it enough? Can you grow that cup so that you can absorb more?

Welcome to the concept of adaptive capacity, or, as I like to call it, 'Mindset X'. This is one of the more subtle ideas in this book, so I want to make sure you understand exactly what I'm talking about. Perhaps

I'll start by explaining when you need to draw on your capacity to adapt.

As a leader, you're used to solving problems. 'Putting out fires' is part of the day-to-day.

Some problems have clear solutions. Say someone leaves your team; you need to replace them. While finding the right person might be tricky, depending on the role, the way to go about it is pretty straightforward. You have a recruitment process to follow with people to help you along the way. Backfilling a role is not new territory. No need to adapt here.

Other situations are more complicated. I worked on an acquisition that required integrating new tech and migrating a lot of data. We needed to consult and work with a lot of experts, carefully identify interdependencies to reduce the risk of outages, scrutinise business continuity plans, and so on. Complicated, yes, but within our existing capacity.

Some situations are chaotic. When my husband had an accident, I was first on the scene. There was blood all over the pavement. Without even thinking, I whipped my top off and used it to apply pressure to stop the bleeding. There was no time to think, no *time* for adaptive behaviour.

By now you may have twigged that I'm leaning into the Cynefin framework (a nod to Dave Snowden). Yep, you've rumbled me. But if you're familiar with it—great—what I'm trying to get across should be clear.

In this practice, I'm talking about complex problems and situations. I have a child with a dynamic nervous system disability. The research on it is limited. There's no clear, existing process to follow. There are no experts to consult to help me create a complicated plan. The chaos cannot be controlled with a pressure bandage. It's complex. The unknowns are unknown and I have learnt the limits of illusions of control. It's through my individual growth as a leader that I can face this complexity and look for the next step to take.

Complex situations are unpredictable and full of moving parts. In the absence of clear answers, you must experiment your way forward. Do a little gentle probing, evaluate the outcome of that probing, probe a little more, and evaluate some more. And on it goes. Take baby steps into the fog, illuminating just a little of the path. The areas of change, strategy and communication often have complex problems. This is the world of VUCA and emerging practices. To survive in this alien world, you must build your capacity to adapt—your Mindset X.

Adaptive capacity is about expansion, but it's not about doing more. I want you to be open to experimentation when dealing with a complex situation. In fact, I want experimentation to be more than okay—I want experimentation to be THE WAY. This is often the mindset of the start-up world; teams experiment their way forward and fast fails are the norm. Adaptive capacity is what science requires, as hypotheses are formed and tested, sometimes fail and sometimes work, and continue to be refined and nudge closer to truth and facts as the variables are identified. It's about discovering, probing, sensing and responding. Sometimes the most obvious solution is not the right one.

You need adaptive capacity so that you can deal with complex situations as and when they appear. As a leader, wanting to fix things is your default mode, but without a strong Mindset X, you run the risk of applying the wrong solutions. For example, you may jump straight to a technical solution. And that's fine if a technical solution is what you need. But this is about more than taking a deep breath, steadying yourself and identifying whether the problem facing you requires a spanner or a wrench. When a problem cannot be identified, you may have to invent new tools. It's difficult to leave the hammer in the toolbox when the temptation is to take action, but adaptive capacity will allow you to sit still and keep your hands in your lap. When you need to invent new tools, it will give you the space and courage to do that.

There is a story related in the book *The Power of Habit* by Charles Duhigg about a US Army major who was dealing with frequent, violent riots in a small city in Iraq in 2003. The obvious solution was to use bombs, guns and soldiers to physically stop the rioting. But after watching videotapes of how the riots unfolded, the major tried non-violent solutions. The one that worked was a civic ordinance banning food trucks from operating in plazas. When the restless, angry crowd got hungry, instead of turning to the food trucks that had set up to cash in on the situation, they went home for dinner. Problem solved—in the most unexpected way—by an army major who had a strong Mindset X—the capacity to adapt.

Not knowing where you are or where to turn or what the next step is can lead to increased anxiety, despair and burnout, which undermines productivity and collaboration and can prevent sound decisions. But simply acknowledging that the future is unknown is helpful. Powerful, in fact. It's huge. Don't dismiss this. The seeds of our future are around us today. Learning to make sense of what is happening now is the first step into that future. It's essential for growth.

The future is approaching fast, and the pace of change today is fast. But is that a bad thing? Sometimes I don't think it's fast enough. When we look at how the world of work, healthcare and education systems need to change for disability and neurodivergent accessibility and inclusion, or how slow we have been in Australia to take a stand on domestic violence and racism, the change is not nearly fast enough. How many more women have to die at the hands of their partner before real change happens? Adaptive capacity can help speed up the pace of change. We won't need endless reports, enquiries and studies; we will be able to jump in and start experimenting our way forward *immediately*.

Knowing that you're in a complex situation helps give you a path, which provides relief and comfort. As you build your Mindset X, your cup will expand.

You will have a greater capacity to deal with complexity, ambiguity and uncertainty; you will be able to hold multiple perspectives; you will mature and become wiser. Not more knowledgeable, but wiser. Instead of searching for answers, you will ask more questions. This is not about measurable skills or capabilities; it's a mindset. And there's a real 'X factor' to this concept. That's why I call it 'Mindset X'.

Making it work

First, you must learn to have compassion for yourself. You will be vulnerable as you grope your way through the darkness. Sometimes you take the wrong turn and have to backtrack. But there's no shame here. Don't judge yourself for these perceived failures; they're the mark of courage.

Building Mindset X is not something you can put on your to-do list, because it can't be learnt by reading fancy textbooks or watching a YouTube clip. It's something you learn by being in it. When I grow leaders in our leadership development programs, we build and strengthen their Mindset X using their real work scenarios and challenges. It has to be experiential learning and has to be contextually relevant. Growth happens in the doing. This is about awareness as much as learning. Start by simply being aware and welcoming opportunities to test and grow your capacity. And don't force it. Like experimenting your way forward in a complex situation, build your capacity gradually, starting with what is required for your current role.

One thing you can do is practise active reflection. Active reflection is a deliberate and purposeful process of examining our experiences, thoughts and actions to gain insights, make meaning, and facilitate learning and growth. We learn from having a new experience, but we learn more by reflecting on the experience—our feelings, thinking habits and actions. This provides an opportunity for change, growth and better performance.

FIGURE 7 Active Reflection

Experience shapes us. Actively reflecting on that experience is like betting 'double or nothing'. We learn the lesson our experience gives us, but reflecting on it supercharges our growth.

Here's how to practise active reflection:

- Think of an experience that has shaped you in your life. It doesn't have to be work related.

- What was challenging about your experience? What did you learn at the time?

- Looking back on the experience, what are you now aware of?

- What would you do differently?

Having a practice of active reflection is one way to develop our thinking and help us see things in a new way. Personally, I like to keep a log of how I've changed my mind and of things I've learnt to see in a new way. I've made it into a game for myself where the objective is to try to add as many items to the log as possible. In the last decade or two, I've changed my mind about many things. For example, I used to stand on the altar of science. Evidence, fact and objectivity were hugely important to me, especially after studying psychology at university. But when I was hit in the face with the limitations and constraints of available research, I grew to understand the value and need to actively seek and listen to lived experience. I also used to think all human behaviour was within our conscious control. Now I know that our environment and nervous systems also have a role to play.

You can try it too...

In the last two years, name three things you now see in a new way, how the shift happened and what it now means for you as you go about work and life.

1.

2.

3.

Mindset X is a superpower. It's not a skillset. It's not what you know but how you know what you know. It's how you think, and how you handle uncertainty, stress and pressure. It's listening to what you're thinking and separating that from how you're feeling so you can do something with it. It's not the tools in the tool kit, or the knowledge or the skills, but the capacity to 'be more'. And it is possible to grow that capacity. To move towards excellence and achieve the transformational outcomes the world and organisations need NOW, we need to press on that growth pedal and invest more in developing leaders to 'be more'. This will make work work for you.

INDIVIDUAL
PERFORMANCE

KNOW YOUR
STRESS LANGUAGE

*Your stress language: Know
it early, de-escalate fast, and
maintain peak performance.*

I HAD a coaching session with the middle manager of a busy tech start-up. The meeting was in his office. I knocked. The door was flung open by a puce-complexioned ogre with steam belching from its ears and torrents of sweat gushing from every available pore. Stepping inside the office, I manoeuvred carefully around the rising floodwaters of perspiration and opened my mouth to say hello. Before I could get any words out, the creature before me, whom I assumed was the lovely client I always enjoyed working with, commenced a rant. I couldn't quite fathom the topic, but his spiel consisted of approximately seventy per cent expletives, including many charmingly placed c-combs. I wasn't frightened. He didn't seem aggressive, just—worked up. I listened patiently for several minutes, noting the more imaginative swear words and mentally filing them away for future use. Meanwhile, I studied him carefully. The veins in his face were popping, but I knew he didn't use Botox. There was no alcohol on his breath; he hadn't had a big night. What was up? I continued to listen, nodding at appropriate intervals, as he continued to vent and get something out of this 'therapeutic complaining'. Then he hit the eye of the storm. A moment of silence. I spoke.

'Sounds stressful,' I suggested.

The ogre, who I was now quite sure was indeed the beautiful client I knew well, looked perplexed.

'No, no, I'm fine. How are you?'

His answer surprised me. It was pretty clear that he was stressed, but when he said he was fine, he was being completely honest—I believe he really meant it. He just couldn't see what I could see.

Covid wasn't the first pandemic of the twenty-first century—stress is also a worldwide problem. In a global study conducted by Qualtrics, forty-two per cent of respondents reported a decline in mental health.[8] Specifically:

- 67% are experiencing increased stress,
- 57% are experiencing increased anxiety,
- 54% are emotionally exhausted,
- 53% are sad,

---

8   https://www.qualtrics.com/blog/confronting-mental-health/

- 50% are irritable,
- 28% are having trouble concentrating,
- 20% are taking longer to finish tasks,
- 15% are having trouble thinking, and
- 12% are challenged to juggle their responsibilities.

Wow... If that impressive list doesn't indicate an epidemic of stress, I don't know what does. And this probably isn't news to you. Stress can even follow you into retirement. When my kids were young, I sometimes asked my dad to look after my hyper-active son for a bit. He would typically say yes, but one day I didn't choose my timing well. Dad had just come back from the bank and was, not surprisingly, in a disgruntled mood. In answer to my request he declared, 'I am retired now, I cannot have any more stress in my life.'

But jokes aside, you can't just wait for stress to go away. Because it's not going away. It's not going away because the stress provokers are not going away. Our tech-enabled world is only exacerbating this problem. As AI takes over more mundane tasks, we will lose more of the 'brain breaks' those tasks gave us. It makes more sense to become masterful in managing stress and finding accommodations that suit our needs.

But do you know when you're stressed? Or are you like my poor client and experiencing dangerous levels of stress without realising it? What was going on with my client that day was that he couldn't read his own signs. He didn't know his stress language.

The language of stress is all about the ways people show they're stressed. It's different for everyone and can turn up in how we act, feel and think, and in physical signs and coping habits. Stressful behaviours are things like procrastinating, being defensive or aggressive, getting less tolerant, or just shutting down. Feelings can include apathy, overwhelm, or being detached and not really present. Stressful thoughts might mean being forgetful, stuck in a mental loop, fixated on certain things, or finding it hard to think clearly. Physically, stress can show up as an upset stomach, eye twitches, loss of appetite, grinding teeth, or being tearful. As for coping mechanisms, they can be negative, like binge eating, endlessly scrolling on your phone, or biting your nails. But they can also be positive, like going for a run or doing some other vigorous exercise.

You might argue that stress is good, that without that spark, urgency and adrenaline you won't meet your deadlines or find the energy you need for a powerful presentation. And that's true—up to a point.

Let's take a closer look at your relationship with stress. That is, your performance level against the amount of stress you have at a certain time. The Yerkes-Dodson Performance and Stress Curve has been around since 1906. The curve features five stress zones, ranging from zone 1, where you're bored, inactive or sleeping, to zone 5, where you might experience exhaustion, fatigue and emotional disturbances such as anxiety, panic attacks, depression and burnout. The ideal place to dwell is zone 2—the performance zone. But what I'm concerned with here is zone 4—the survival zone. Here, adrenaline and cortisol begin pumping through your body, which is fine—for a bit. Normally, these hormones spike and then go back down to their set point to repair and recover. The challenge is when stress provokers come at you constantly and the stress just builds and builds and builds. Your body doesn't have time to get back down to that happy place—the set point where it achieves homeostasis. This is a big problem. If you stay in the survival zone for extended periods, you'll tip over into zone 5. This is why you need to know when you're in zone 4—so that you can take steps to de-escalate and get back to the sweet spot of zone 2, which is where your performance is optimised. If my client had known his stress language, he could have given that performance pedal a push before he boiled over from zone 4 to zone 5.

Naming something is powerful. If you know your stress language, you can de-escalate your stress before it becomes critical. This helps you stay mentally and physically healthy, which improves your productivity and performance. It also prevents the stress from becoming contagious—both at home and at work. And believe me, stress is just as contagious as the other twenty-first-century pandemic. Becoming fluent in your personal stress language will also help you to articulate your stress in a constructive way, which influences those around you to do the same and helps create an uplifting environment where emotional maturity is valued.

Making it work

To learn your stress language, think back to times when you were stressed and try to remember the signs you were showing. You can also tune in to moments when you *are* stressed, although this can be tricky because you have to get in touch with yourself when you're in a heightened state. The key is to notice and name the feeling, action, thought or bodily experience. Don't name and shame, just notice, sign and name it.

I use the acronym FATE, which stands for feel, act, think, experience. Using this acronym, you can articulate how stress makes you feel, how it makes you act, how it makes you think and how the experience feels physically.

For example, when stressed, you might FEEL:

- Angry
- Frustrated
- Flustered
- Frightened

When stressed, you might ACT:

- Impulsively
- Frantically
- Unwisely
- Too slowly

When stressed, you might THINK:

- Rapidly
- Slowly
- Unclearly
- Not at all

When stressed, you might EXPERIENCE:

- A racing pulse
- Knots in your stomach
- Rapid breathing
- A red, sweaty face

F	Feel
A	Act
T	Think
E	Experience

FIGURE 8 The FATE Test

Once you become familiar, and eventually fluent, in your stress language, you'll know when you're stressed. Sometimes just noticing the stress and acknowledging it is enough to bring it down. But if you need more structured help, you can create a personalised stress circuit breaker.[9] This is something I work on with my coaching clients because it needs to be highly personalised. I helped one general manager create a circuit breaker that involved spending time on her special interests. For another, it was about regulating their nervous system with somatic exercises. Everybody is different, but there are solutions out there if you're willing to spend the time and find the help you need to create effective circuit breakers.

Learning your stress language is the first step to bringing down your overall stress levels. When your stress levels are in a safe zone, you will be happier and healthier, and this will feed into your ability to perform. When you can perform at your best, you are on the road to excellence, and you will find that work works much better for you.

---

9   The term 'stress circuit breaker' was coined by my colleague Valerie Judge, Director of Rose Phoenix Health. She introduced me to stress language and her stress circuit breaker at the Melbourne Accelerator Program when she was working with founders on wellbeing for entrepreneurs. Together (and independently), Val and I have gone on to support people to understand how stress shows up for them and what they can do about it, and have run many workshops together to help people manage stress and prevent burnout.

HONOUR NEEDS,
NOT NORMS

Honour needs, not norms: Understand that meeting personal needs leads to better performance outcomes.

I WAS booked to deliver a keynote address at a conference being held at a TAFE in my home town of Melbourne, and was delighted that my session was turning out to be popular. So popular that we had to change the venue from a comfortable, sound-proofed auditorium, purpose-built for hosting presentations, to the cavernous, clattering student cafeteria, purpose-built for feeding hungry hordes of unwashed uni students. It was not a venue I would have chosen.

Changes had to be improvised. We found screens to hide the coke cans and pies piled up in the display case, but the audio situation was disastrous and it was impossible to get everybody's attention without a mic. 'Hands on heads, everybody!' might work in a primary school classroom to pump up the energy, but not here.

Then a helpful man in the audience got to his feet and issued a long, loud, ear-piercing whistle. I was impressed. And grateful... because it worked. In an instant, eyes and ears were turned towards me. But before diving into my presentation, I asked the helpful gentleman if he would oblige with further whistles if I began to lose my audience again. He kindly agreed. A few ripples of laughter went around the room, and I opened my mouth to begin—only to be interrupted. A woman stood, waved her arms to get my attention, and stated that if another high-pitched whistle were to assault her ears, she would leave. She meant it. She was not happy. Her needs were not being met.

We all have needs, which vary greatly from person to person. You might have heard of Maslow's hierarchy of needs. This puts survival needs and safety needs at the bottom and moves through four more levels before hitting self-actualisation at the top. But I believe there's more to be explored here. In our world of work, we need to extend our understanding beyond this and recognise that many of us have cognitive, social, sensory and communication needs too. This applies both to you as a leader, and to the individuals you lead. And if these needs aren't met, we can't perform at our best. Work won't work for us.

An example of a **cognitive** need is how much time you need to process an idea or solution. How quickly do you go from idea to action? Some people are quick, some are slower. Neither is good or bad; it depends on the task, circumstances and your brain.

Cognitive	**Social**
Sensory	**Communication**

FIGURE 9 The 4 Types of Needs

A **social** need could be how much alone time you need. Do you need to do things by yourself across the workweek? Or are you happy working in a chatty team environment from morning to night? Perhaps you feel more social in the mornings, in which case you might prefer to schedule one-on-one meetings first thing.

Then there are **sensory** needs, which are sometimes difficult to understand. An example is people who concentrate better if their hands are moving, which is the case for some neurodivergent leaders I work with. A partner in a law firm once told me he needed the noise of a fan to concentrate.

Communication needs are easier to understand. For example, my father has trouble listening to people who include a lot of colour and 'fluff' that's not critical to the key point. As a child, when I explained something to him, he would often say, 'Get to the point darling, I'm losing interest!' It sounds rude, but it wasn't (and this happens to this day!) in our family. I understood his need, and would simply thank him for the reminder, quicken the pace of my story and cut to the chase.

And that's the key here—everybody's needs are different. It's important to understand that different needs don't make people less, just different. The world turns more smoothly when we honour people's needs, not just the norms. When I delivered my keynote in the TAFE cafeteria, the challenge was around both sensory and communication needs. Many people in the audience were having difficulty paying attention to me; the sound quality was poor and the environment was full of distractions. I thought that ear-piercing whistle had done the trick until the poor woman at the back of the cafeteria complained about it. At the first break, I made a beeline for her. She helped me understand that she was tired, she had a lot of stress in her life, and she was sensitive to noise. She wanted to hear my presentation, but her 'threat' to leave was not a threat at all. She was simply stating a fact: she could not tolerate high-pitched whistling, and if there was going to be a lot of it, she would have to leave. Sadly, some eye-rolling in the audience suggested that people thought she was just grumpy. But when I spoke to her I discovered that categorisation was wrong. I was glad I had a chance to apologise and grateful for this learning experience.

I'm not talking about preferences here. The audience member who wanted quiet didn't simply *prefer* it, she *needed* it. Unlike preferences, needs are hard requirements. While our neurobiology shapes behaviour to some extent, so do our environment and working conditions. When our needs are not met by the environment, it affects our behaviour, which affects our performance. Suppressed needs can cause disconnection, physical pain and stress, and lead to burnout.

Research confirms that unmet or suppressed needs can have a negative impact on a person's overall performance at work.[10] When organisations take individuals' needs and personal characteristics into account, the performance of teams has been found to improve by up to sixty-five per cent.[11] If you need silence for deep work, your work will be less effective in a noisy environment. If someone needs visual information to take the load off their brain, they will find it hard to concentrate during a Power-Point-free presentation. If someone needs to not hear ear-piercing whistles, they cannot listen to a presentation punctuated by them. The fact is, we can't

---

10 Andersson, M. A., Walker, M. H., & Kaskie, B. P. (2019). Strapped for Time or Stressed Out? Predictors of Work Interruption and Unmet Need for Workplace Support Among Informal Elder Caregivers. *Journal of Aging and Health, 31*(4), 631-651. https://doi.org/10.1177/0898264317744920

11 Valkovicova, Jana, and Tracey Tokuhama-Espinosa. Performance Management in Neurodivergent Teams. (2021).

do our best if our needs aren't met. You can't bring your best voice to an Uber karaoke session if you have to hold your breath because everybody has BO!

We need to be responsive to, and respectful of both our own and other people's needs and adjust our environment and work practices accordingly. But this is not easy, as people's needs change over time and sometimes our differing needs conflict, as in the TAFE cafeteria that day. But don't worry, you don't have to be across all of this. Just developing some awareness and accommodating needs as best you can will make things run more smoothly. And when you give yourself a break in regard to your own needs—when you honour and accommodate them and stop trying to stifle them—your own performance will peak.

Making it work

I gave you a few examples of needs above—people who need silence for deep work, others who benefit from fidget toys, and those who cherish the visual support of a PowerPoint. You can start learning to honour needs, not norms, simply by becoming aware of these things. You can also normalise having specific needs by role modelling. For example, sometimes I tell my audience: 'I've been in back-to-back meetings, and I do my best thinking on the move, so I'm going to stand for this session. '

You can also be a bit more proactive and show

you're open to providing accommodations for people's needs. For example, I offer fidget tools at the start of our training sessions for anyone who likes to use them to support cognitive processing and emotional regulation. (I will never forget the general manager who selected an eggplant stress ball. We all know what the eggplant emoji looks like, right? A few giggles went around the room when she proceeded to roll the squishy eggplant sensuously in her hands and shape its head just so!) It's also important to not force participation or socialisation in workshops. No matter how much or what type of support you provide, there will be participants who need to be less involved.

When I conduct workshops I also send out an email beforehand, which invites participants to share any and all accommodations and supports they may require to maximise their level of comfort and performance during the session. I like to be explicit in that email. I explain that I work with a number of neurodivergent senior leaders who do their best thinking with a fidget spinner in hand, a coaching client who doodles and doesn't often make eye contact, and others who need regular opportunities to stand and walk because of their physical needs. I also explain that there are people who benefit from receiving as much information as possible before attending workshops, as they prefer to do their thinking alone and before entering a group setting. The responses to this email are, of course, entirely private, but it allows me to be better prepared. It also helps create a secure environment where people feel safe to express their needs.

These are approaches and practices I've developed over time, and I continue to increase my awareness, understanding and acceptance of people's varying needs. I know that you can too. I believe we must work collectively to advance our world of work to become 'neurodiversity-affirming', meaning that all brains belong and we see difference, not disorder. This will help to make work work for everyone. The path to becoming neurodiversity-affirming as an individual and as a leader is an important one. As a leader, you will come to know your people better, know their needs better and be able to make tweaks. It's a work in progress, which is just fine, and it's also a step towards excellence.

MANAGE
YOUR STATE

Energy sync:
Match your state to the moment
to maximise your impact.

WHAT STATE are you in right now? No, I don't want to know if you're in Queensland or Victoria or Tasmania, or maybe somewhere in the US. I'm asking—*what's* your state? What's your vibe? Your energy? Take a moment to look inside and experience your whole self—your emotions, mind and body. What's it like in there? Are you buzzing magnetically, oozing charisma through your pores? Are there sparks igniting, bright enough to light up the room? Or is it dark and dank in there; are you a human energy drain, sapping the life out of anyone who comes close to you?

Everybody has a state, which is the whole of a person at the moment. A person's state can be felt by both them and the people around them. As humans, we have a whole-body experience in the presence of other people. But it's not an energy expressed through body language, tone of voice or any aspect of our demeanour. It's a force that can be felt without any sensory input. You've probably had that experience of someone coming into a room, and while they're just on your periphery, you can sense that they're angry.

This is rooted in our biology. Our heart's magnetic field is up to 5,000 times more powerful than the magnetic field of the brain and can be detected up to three metres away. We transmit signals in a similar way to other animals—as vibrations that travel through the airwaves.[12] I can sometimes identify a person's state with my eyes tightly shut. This might have happened to you too. If you've never thought about this, perhaps try it and see. It's not unusual to know intuitively what a person's state is.

And why is this important? To perform at your best and do great, you need to make sure your state matches the moment. When your inner state is the wrong one, everything can go wrong. For example, I went to a wedding recently. Everybody was happy, charged, and full of joy for the couple about to step into wedded bliss. Then the celebrant arrived, and it was like she had turned down the sun. It felt more like a wake than a wedding. Her state was the wrong

---

12 Rosch, P.J., & Markov, M.S. (Eds.). (2004). Bioelectromagnetic Medicine (1st ed.). CRC Press. https://doi.org/10.3109/9780203021651

state for the moment; it was jarring, and it took a bit of time (and a few sips of champagne) to get our happy vibe back.

Then there was a workshop I conducted for a pilot program using VR to help senior managers understand employees with marginalised traits, such as Indigenous or neurodivergent employees or employees who had experienced racism. It was designed to be confronting, to make the participants uncomfortable in a way that would encourage them to reflect and contemplate and ultimately feel inspired to find solutions. I arrived off the back of a string of motivational sessions and was upbeat, energetic, full of smiles and buzzing with energy. My vibe was all wrong for the serious and important subject we were learning about. Everybody felt uncomfortable, but not in the constructive way I had hoped for. It took effort to shift my state and get things back on track.

Your inner state needs to match the mood of the moment. You need to emit the right energy to nail your performance and get the outcome you want. The state you should be in when announcing redundancies is not the one you want for a keynote address, and vice versa. Being in the wrong state confuses and weakens the message. Being in the right state makes your presentation more effective and your presence stronger. Being in the right state will help you mobilise change, inspire others, get customers' buy-in, and build trust and connection.

Changing our state can support people struggling under pressure. When our state is calm, we can calm someone who is feeling overwhelmed through a process called coregulation. This allows you to lower stress levels in a workplace context. You do this through your state, not your words and actions. It works the other way too—you can make people excited, inspired and energised when that's required.

A person's state is contagious, which is at the heart of what makes it effective. And you can't fake it; it must be real. People around you will detect your state without any concrete cues. No matter how much you try to control your body language, tone of voice and demeanour, if your state is the wrong one for the moment, people will know you're faking it, that you're 'performing'. Your state has to be authentic. I'll say that again because it's important—your state must be authentic. It must be fit for purpose.

State is also temporary—a phenomenon of a moment—and while it can't be faked, it can be deliberately and consciously shifted. This is what I mean when I talk about state 'management'. It's not easy, but being able to shift your state is a learnable skill. State management is something I often coach leaders on, especially when they want to become more effective public speakers.

In the world of work, I believe there are three basic states you need to embody at different times:

1   **Inspiring**. As a leader, it's your role to create the conditions for excellence. Leading change well is part and parcel of the gig and so you need to be able to inspire others.

2   **Self-assured/confident/serious**. Leaders have

to lead. The organisation needs to succeed. If you're unsure or hesitant about your decisions, where you're taking your team or where the organisation is going, you won't get their buy-in.

3 **Calm and supportive**. When things go pear-shaped, everybody takes their cues from you. If you panic or lose your cool, they will too. But if you keep it together, you'll help everybody get over the obstacles.

When you're in one state, but need to be in another, you need to shift it. For example, if you're just about to step out in front of an audience and deliver a motivating speech and your current state is calm and supportive, you probably need to shift your state to inspiring. It's hard to do that without practice, but practice will make it easier.

Making it work

When it comes to learning state management, I've found it useful to draw on lessons from the performing arts. Actors use many techniques to prepare before stepping onto the stage or in front of a camera. According to *Backstage* magazine, there are as many as thirteen different techniques.[13] The most well known and possibly the most intense is the Method

---

13 https://www.backstage.com/magazine/article/acting-techniques-mean-1534/

technique developed by Lee Strasberg. A key technique of the Method is emotional recall, in which actors draw on real experiences from their own lives to inform their performances. This is useful in state management because it taps into authentic emotions and is not mere performance or mimicry.

When you need to shift your current state, you can tap into the memory of being in a more appropriate state. Shifting your state is easier when you have a 'bank' of emotions and sensations to draw on. To do this, find some time to think back to when you were in a specific state. Go deep here. How did it feel? Bring the image of that time into your mind and feel all the feelings. Really try to embody those feelings. It's an emotional experience, but try to take it further and get your whole body buzzing in the right state. By practising like this, you will find it easier to shift states at will.

When I need a high-energy, inspiring state, I recall my experiences at music festivals. Those are times when I have an open heart, and I feel super happy and elevated. I smile so much that my cheeks hurt the next day. I feel that buzz and glow around me and dance like no one is watching. There's no inhibition. So before I go on stage for a keynote, I recall that moment at a festival or concert when the beat drops and the crowd goes wild. I love the energy of those moments. I bottle it up, and it becomes my fragrance of choice—my signature scent that I spray just before I go on stage.

You won't always need a high-energy state. You

might need to feel calm, but strong and confident before an important event. I had a friend who was invited to do the coin toss before a major football game. She called me in a panic and said, 'Louise, I've got stage fright. And I don't even have to speak! How do you get up on stage and actually talk? If you could give me one hot tip, what would it be?'

People ask me this sort of thing all the time. It's a common scenario with my coaching clients. Maybe they have to give a presentation—large or small—or go into a critical meeting or attend a tough job interview. They've done half their preparation; they've got their messages, their notes and their materials in order. They know what they want to say. Yet they're still in a state of panic. So, are they really prepped and ready to go? No. They also need to practise their state. If you haven't prepped and practised your state, you're half baked! And we know what happens if you half cook a chicken—you'll be back in the loo in no time.

This is the three-step process I shared with my friend to help get her into the right state for the coin toss, stay calm, feel strong and banish stage fright.

1 **Prepare**. Work out the state you need to be in and identify a memory you can use. My friend needed to be strong, confident and self-assured, so she recalled going into her under-twenty-one basketball grand final undefeated. 'I walked on that court feeling so good. So strong,' she told me.

2 **Plan**. Plan what you will do if any of your worries

manifest. In my friends' case, she was worried about failing to catch the coin. If that happened, she decided she would just laugh and pick it up.

3 **Perform**. Connect with the emotional memory of the state you identified in Step 1 just before you have to step out and 'perform'. Remember that you've prepared for this, and you're ready. Just tap into your emotional memory and spring into action.

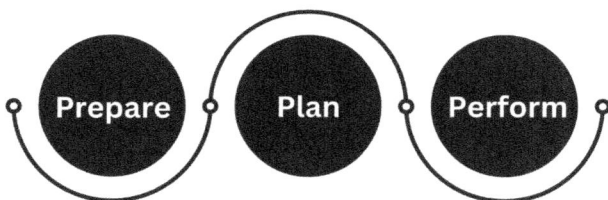

FIGURE 10 The 3 Steps of State Management

These steps can easily be adapted for any situation.

State management is important, and it could be the push on the performance pedal you need to start doing great. When you start doing great, this will spill over and boost your growth and wellbeing as well. The key is preparation. Yes, you can just 'wing it', and there is a time for that. But even impromptu actors prepare. They might not have a script to read, but they need to be in the right state before going on stage if their performance is going to be effective. As my clever business buddy Col Fink says, 'You need to spend more time preparing yourself than preparing your stuff.' Preparing yourself by finding the right state for the right moment will give you an edge of excellence that other leaders may lack.

PART 2

TEAM PRACTICES

WELCOME TO PART 2, where we step beyond practices at the individual level and move on to the team-based practices.

Teams are the basic units of an organisation. An organisation can be a single team or contain dozens or even hundreds of teams. Those teams are made up of people in individual roles who work together interdependently. Team members rely on each other. They have to work together to achieve their goals. A team is more than just a group of people.

Teams are critical, but they sometimes feel like sandwich filling. There can be issues with cohesion caused by a lack of alignment among the people making up the team. There can be issues in the other direction too. Teams can become insular and lose their connection to the organisation's why and purpose.

The practices in this section are a bit like the work I do with teams to achieve 'real shifts' for them. They might take longer than a day to implement and will take longer to produce results than some of the individual practices. But they're all important. They will help your teams become the solid centre that holds the organisation together.

Remember that while these practices are laid out for you, the leader, to read and digest and suggest, the application must be at the team level. It's not solely a leader's job to 'fix' a team. As a leader, you need to guide teams, not grill them or bark orders at them. Leading a team is about supporting its members to become self-sufficient and more self-leading while they align their team goals to the broader organisational strategy. A healthy, growing, productive team is a team that works on itself from the inside out.

Also remember that there's no trade-off between performance, growth and wellbeing. There's no reason why you can't have all three. In fact, you must. The key is to press all three pedals and do the right moves at the right time to create excellence. And while these practices are set out according to the three pedals, boosting one will have ripple effects that enhance all three. The practices in Part 2 are really about how teams can work 'better together'. If you implement them, you'll have a team that is feeling good, doing great and getting better.

TEAM
WELLBEING

TEAM TETRIS

*Team tetris: Rotate and move team
tasks for ultimate team wellbeing.*

WHEN WAS the last time you looked at your job
description? Let me guess—was it the day you
analysed the key competencies required for the
role, making sure you could score points for the
behavioural-based questions they would ask in the
interview? In other words, the day you applied for
the job? Very possibly. And are you now doing the
job that was described in the position description?
Did you think you were taking a senior leadership
position, only to find that you have no EA and spend
half your day being a leader and the other half hunt-
ing down meeting rooms? Were you recruited for
your 'energy and enthusiasm' only to find your
role was to boost morale? Were you promised a
'dynamic work environment', only to find no one had
a clue what was going on? A quick perusal of the

Dilbert comic strip tells us that job ads and position descriptions are often the butt of jokes.

Now, I'm not knocking them—position descriptions are a necessity. But they only tell part of the story. They paint the high-level picture, not the day-to-day reality of working life. They're about responsibilities, not the *experience* of the job. As a leader, I want to get you thinking beyond people in roles with accompanying job descriptions; I want you to start thinking about how the work is done in a way that supports wellbeing. I call this Team Tetris.

I came up with this term when I was working as a team coach at strategy days and offsites. Often the challenge was working out how to deliver outcomes in a cost-cutting environment while protecting the team's wellbeing. You may have heard of the Buy, Build, Borrow concept. In this traditional approach, there are three ways to increase the capacity of your team. 'Buy' means budgeting to increase the size of the team. 'Build' means increasing the capacity of the team through professional development or other means. And 'Borrow' essentially means using contractors, which is easier with the rise of the gig economy. But there is a fourth 'B'—Balance—which means reconfiguring and rejigging, and that's what we're talking about here. It's about doing more with less. Or doing more with what you've got. It's also the option that protects the team's wellbeing.

In my work as a team coach, I noticed that the best teams had pieces that fitted together and complemented each other perfectly. It was like Tetris pieces slotting in 'just so'. Sometimes you had to rotate a piece a little or move it around to get the right fit, but when you did, everything clicked. So now, when I work with leaders and teams, I think of my work as helping them play a game of Team Tetris.

Work comprises not just tasks, but people and thinking. It includes the amount of work we do as well as the type of work. Team Tetris involves looking at ways to alter these things to suit people's needs and strengths. It's about changing the job to suit the person wherever possible.

Team Tetris can be better understood by looking at an example, in this case the phenomenon of job sharing. In the most basic approach, job sharing means that two (or possibly more) employees are in the same role but work on different days. Joe Bloggs files the invoices from Monday to Wednesday, and Jane Bloggs files the invoices on Thursday and Friday. But it can be so much more sophisticated than this.

I was brought in to assist with a pilot program for a company trying to embed job-share arrangements into their culture so they could attract better-quality candidates. In this case, two women were sharing one job, and the arrangement had been in place for about a year. The handover of duties was going smoothly enough, and the work was getting done, but they wanted to take things further.

The two women sharing the job came from different backgrounds and had different strengths and challenges. They were also at different stages of their careers and had different ambitions for the future. Despite sharing a single job, they had never met, let alone had time to step back and consider their values, strengths and what they needed from their role to maximise work/life balance and support their future ambitions.

When we're playing Team Tetris, we're tweaking the way the work is designed and divvied up. So this isn't about a formal contract but about internal agreements. Agreement on how duties are shared should come from a place of mutual understanding. For example, if one person has more interest in moving up the corporate chain, perhaps they should take the lead in cross-functional meetings. This grows the person and prepares them for future roles. It's important that people play to their strengths, but it's equally important that nobody 'taps out'. Perhaps one employee is a strong public speaker, and the other has a lot of anxiety about this. Should the stronger speaker shoulder the work that requires public speaking? Not necessarily—perhaps there's a growth opportunity here for the more anxious person. It's best to make a deliberate decision; people shouldn't find themselves landed with work by default. And beyond the employees involved, any job-sharing arrangement must be seamless and work for the whole team and the stakeholders. We're pressing the growth pedal here, but we don't want to take our foot off the wellbeing and performance pedals.

Tasks are performed by individuals. Work is done by a team. The example above involves just two people, but the same principles can be applied across a whole team. In a perfect game of Team

Tetris, every team member plays to their strengths, is supported in their lesser strengths, and is stretched the right amount and in the right direction. A perfectly balanced team, in which each member is a perfect fit for their consciously designed work roles, hums with harmony and contentment. Sounds ambitious? Yes, it is. You have to be clever about this and willing to adapt. And while it's not easy, the benefits are many.

It's important to understand that this is not just a question of evening out lumpy workloads. It's common to see teams where a few members are getting smashed while others are cruising along. I often see this in companies where there's an element of seasonality in the workload. I also see leaders proactively making short-term moves to even out that workload. This is a good start, and while it's necessary, it's not sufficient. Team Tetris is about intentionally making moves, not as a reactive strategy to balance workloads, but as a proactive step to support wellbeing.

Well-designed work provides fulfilment, while a poor fit between a person and their work role is a leading factor in burnout. Research carried out among healthcare workers in 2020 discovered that seventy-eight per cent of employees in poorly fitting jobs reported exhaustion, seventy-six per cent experienced cynicism and seventy-five per cent experienced reduced personal accomplishment.[14]

---

14 Cavanaugh, Katelyn J., et al. An examination of burnout predictors: Understanding the influence of job attitudes and environment. *Healthcare*. Vol. 8. No. 4. MDPI, 2020.

Better work/life balance is a clear benefit of consciously designing work to suit the people doing it.

The game of Tetris is about creating full rows with no gaps. When we play Tetris with the work that a team does, it evens out workloads. Putting the right person on the right task means work is completed faster. In turn, this feeds capacity. Employee wellbeing is supported when people are not overloaded. Or, indeed, underloaded. The phenomenon of 'cyberloafing' is a coping mechanism people turn to when they don't have enough to do.[15] One study found that 'work underload' led to fifty-one per cent of employees considering a career change.[16] When you have employees completing all their work in the first five minutes they spend at their desks, only to fill the rest of the day twiddling their thumbs or scrolling on their phones, they'll soon be looking elsewhere for stimulation and satisfaction.

Remember that people want to contribute. In the game of Tetris, four blocks can make up seven different shapes. That's a lot of possibilities and a lot of opportunity to strategically rotate, move and allocate work to give people a chance to extend themselves. In doing this, the experience of work

---

15 Pindek, Shani, Alexandra Krajcevska, and Paul E. Spector. Cyberloafing as a Coping Mechanism: Dealing with Workplace Boredom. *Computers in human behavior* 86 (2018): 147–152. Web.

16 Clemons, Jessica. Investigating work engagement and affective commitment through a multi-dimensional work underload scale, mediated by work-related boredom. (2020).

is enhanced. The team is happier and healthier. Research bears this out. An article published in *Academy of Management* found that 'High-quality work design has positive impacts including enhanced individual/team performance; increased employee wellbeing; positive attitude towards work and improved organisational performance.'[17]

Team Tetris enhances team wellbeing and can even be used to support employees when their wellbeing has been compromised by factors outside their work environment. I worked with a general manager who had taken some time off to support his health and recover from fatigue. In this case, playing Team Tetris involved co-creating a plan with members of his team and sharing it with the broader team when he returned. That plan made it clear that he would slowly transition to work as he recovered, with reduced work load and a lighter mental load. The lighter mental load was critical. The need to constantly make decisions put a high demand on his executive functioning, and this demand would not support his recovery. By working with other leaders and his broader team to rotate and move team tasks, we supported not only the GM's health, but the whole team's wellbeing.

In an increasingly diverse world, where team members bring increasingly diverse strengths, skills

---

17 Parker, Sharon K., Anja Van den Broeck, and David Holman. Work design influences: A synthesis of multilevel factors that affect the design of jobs. *Academy of Management Annals* 11.1 (2017): 267-308.

and ambitions, work design will become even more valuable. Take a moment and ask yourself whether the ways of working that you have inherited are still the best ways of working. Can you afford the opportunity cost of not leaning into the challenge and complexity of Team Tetris? At least give it a try.

This is where Team Tetris comes in.

Making it work

A way to get started on Team Tetris is to set up a workshop to review the team's tasks. Individually, map out how much time is spent on different parts of each member's role. Review what people are good at, motivated by and passionate about in light of how much time they're spending on those things. Then...

Rejig it.

Here are the seven steps for playing Team Tetris:

1 **Start Game**. Set the context and clearly and honestly explain why you want to work with the team to play a little Team Tetris. Top tip: to maintain psychological safety, make the rules explicit. Call out that this is not about restructuring; this is an opportunity to balance workloads, play to your strengths, align work to wellbeing and support growth and career objectives, and so on—whatever is relevant for your team. Also note that changes should only be made when necessary—there might be a lot to do, or there might be a little.

2   **Prepare moves.** Before the workshop, everyone should, individually as a pre-work reflection: a) identify their values, strengths, motivators and interests, b) look at how they currently spend their time and energy at work and c) reflect on what insights this exercise brought out for them.

3   **Understand the board**. Meet 1:1 with everyone to go through their insights. The purpose is just to listen and understand and, if needed, coach and support people to stretch further with their pre-work and insights. N.B. Depending on your team members, you may choose to skip this step, or you may only need to do this the first time you play Team Tetris.

4   **Exchange ideas**. Get everyone together, form small groups and have people share their pre-workshop reflections.

5   **Strategise moves**. As a group, brainstorm small plays and moves to experiment with to rotate and tweak how the work is done.

6   **Place pieces**. Create a plan, some small commitments and experiments to try. Avoid the temptation to come up with a laundry list of changes. This is about small moves.

7   **Tally the score**. After about three weeks, get the team back together and evaluate against the goals that were set at the start. Keep what worked and discard what didn't. Then play again.

Remember that Team Tetris is not set-and-forget. It's something that should become a practice, a play that you make on an ongoing basis. In my experience, teams appreciate this from their leaders and it really boosts engagement.

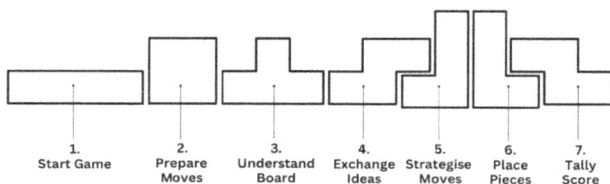

| 1. Start Game | 2. Prepare Moves | 3. Understand Board | 4. Exchange Ideas | 5. Strategise Moves | 6. Place Pieces | 7. Tally Score |

FIGURE 11 Your Team Tetris Play

When all your people are using their strengths, stimulated by their work and supported in their challenges, a sense of calm and satisfaction will descend. People will be in the zone, in flow, in their element—or whatever you like to call it. Team Tetris leads to enhanced job satisfaction, better team performance, and more efficient workflows by aligning individual strengths and interests with team needs. All of that adds up to a quick press on the well-being pedal, and a well team is one in which the work works for everyone and the team is speeding towards excellence.

MEETING
MAKEOVERS

Give your meetings an extreme makeover by decluttering the agenda and adding elements that boost engagement and wellbeing.

MOST WORKPLACES have rituals. A favourite is the birthday celebration in the tea room, when the team has a welcome break from their work and a chance to enjoy a bit of cake and the company of their colleagues in a more social setting. I knew the director of a financial services business who inevitably supplied a slightly squished, plastic-wrapped mud cake he bought from the local supermarket that bore a sticker proudly announcing that it was 'REDUCED TO CLEAR'. He was not exactly strapped for cash and could have easily produced a full-priced, multi-layered continental gateau from an upmarket patisserie, but that's why everybody thought the cheap cake was hilarious. It became a tradition, and whenever a birthday came round, the hunt was on for cheap cake. As the cake got cheaper, the laughs got louder. All of which is a roundabout way to say that rituals have no rules. If cheap cake creates connection among team members, then the cheaper the better. If sharing that cheap cake uplifts people, keep sharing it. Rituals are important because they have meaning; meaning creates momentum, and momentum helps get the proverbial done.

There is one type of ritual, however, that's an exception. You guessed it—meetings. Meetings are the type of ritual I hear about the most in my work with leaders and teams. And not in a good way. Leaders have confided in me that no one participates in their meetings, that the team is just not engaged and that people don't even show up. They tell me they have all these meetings on their calendar, so they go to them, but they don't say anything. Or the meetings turn into a talkfest where nothing gets done. Or the meetings have no point, but they have to go to them and talk because it gives them exposure. I even hear about meetings that could easily be replaced with a single email. How many times have you said, 'I can't get any work done because I'm stuck in meetings all day!'? How is that progressing the work? It's not! If your meetings are more problematic than purposeful, you need a meeting makeover. Maybe even an extreme one.

You know when you're in a bad meeting. People don't contribute. A cone of silence descends. That silence becomes increasingly uncomfortable. People sigh, look longingly at the door or down at their phones. They don't even try to hide the fact they're looking at reels under the table. Or maybe there's a lot of talk, but talk about the wrong things. When a meeting is going badly, you can feel the energy drain from the room. Soon it feels almost impossible to sit upright in your chair. How can a team get anything done when every cell in everybody's body is asleep on the job? And you can bet that draining feeling is going to follow everybody out the door and back to their desks, where they'll try to get back into the groove of doing whatever it was the meeting took them away from—that is, the 'real work'.

The frustration of being prevented from getting things done is obvious, but the real damage goes deeper. It's about wellbeing. Bad meetings damage relationships. When you schedule a meeting and nobody turns up, it hurts your feelings. It's like being stood up on a date. The lack of clarity and progress typical of poorly run meetings creates unnecessary noise and stress. There's no sense of accomplishment, engagement is damaged, purpose and meaning are missing. No one is getting what they need. All this builds up and damages the wellbeing of the whole team.

Let's flip it. Good meetings create connection and therefore build quality relationships. Relationships are a pillar of wellbeing and a team that feels good does good work. Good meetings are energising, they provide clarity and move things forward. People will *want* to come to meetings if they're well run. They will make time for meetings, they will put them in their diary, they will be on time, they will bring their positive energy. That energy will be contagious and team members will be turning cartwheels of joy on their way back to their desks. No more brain-dead zombies littering the corridors after each and every meeting.

It is possible to have meetings like this, and it's not a matter of luck or good fortune. It's about intention and conscious effort. A company that has excelled at creating effective, energising meetings is Yarra Valley Water. As part of their commitment to a hybrid working model, they put time, effort and deep thought into creating guidelines for when, why and how to hold meetings for their key 'Moments That Matter'. Just imagine how refreshing it would be if your team viewed meetings as moments that matter.

Making it work

If you want meetings that move you forward, you may need to give your meetings a makeover. No, I don't mean put lipstick on them. It's more like giving your house a makeover. More like a renovation. I'm sure you've seen those home renovation shows. The first thing they do is show us the 'before'. It's the same with meetings. You need to take a 'before' picture to figure out what's working and what's not. Just like asking the people who live in a house how they'd like to change the floorplan, the décor or the backyard, you need to talk to people who attend the meetings you're making over. The before picture informs the decision on whether to refurbish, renovate or knock down and rebuild. Just like a house, it's about liveability and value. You need to get rid of the mould, the damp—perhaps even some asbestos—all the things that are damaging the wellbeing of the occupants and give them a fresh, clean, functional environment that lets them flourish.

There are many ways to get the 'before' picture prior to making over or renovating your meetings. I've often done this as part of bigger change programs. It can come up in one-on-one research interviews, or through surveys or, if there is psychological safety, it can be workshopped.

One way to get that before picture is to start scoring the effectiveness of meetings. Try introducing a 1-10 or 1-5 rating. Ask the participants, 'How valuable was this meeting? Give me a score from 1-5.' For example, 'My time is wasted' might be a one, while 'Decisions are clear and everyone delivers on their actions' would be a five or a ten, depending on the scale. 'My time is wasted, I don't need to be at this meeting' would be a low score, while 'I get a good return on the investment of my time' would be a high score. I have a number of variables and scoring items I ask participants to give me a rating on. As you go around the room and ask for ratings, pause if somebody gives a low score and have them explain why and what they think could have been done better.

I introduced this technique to meetings I was running in a change management initiative, and rather than alienating staff, other teams began to adopt it. We didn't need to do it for very long before we whipped our meetings into a shape that moved things forward. I'm sure you'll achieve a similar result if you do this in the right spirit.

If you do this, make sure everyone knows that the scoring is to help improve future meetings so they make the best use of everyone's time. It also means that everyone can take accountability for the effectiveness and outcomes of meetings. It should not be a disciplinary or shame-inducing exercise. There's no right or wrong answer and there's no fallout from being honest. It's about respecting everyone's time and getting input into how effective the meeting is.

Scoring meetings in this way might seem confronting, but it's better to have issues out in the open and you'll find that participants value this practice. Also, when you score a meeting like this, you'll find it changes what participants bring into the room, and your meetings will not only become productive, but will be a constructive forum that your team members look forward to taking part in. They will energise, not exhaust, and everybody will be feeling good.

Once you have a before picture, it's important that you put the work into designing future meetings to be more effective. You need to be intentional about this. To help create a better 'after' picture for meetings that need making over or renovating, I'd like to introduce you to what I call the 3 Ds. And no, it's not a bra size. Knowing the fit provides the support you need to move forward. When I've worked with teams to find their perfect fit, people come to meetings prepared and they engage. They see meetings as a way to get their work done, not a weight pulling them down.

Just like giving a house a fresh coat of paint, giving your meetings a fresh 'coat' of purpose will revitalise them. Meetings that move you forward and support wellbeing by energising the team are about three things: direction, discovery and dynamics. **Direction** meetings should focus on strategy and solutions. **Discovery** meetings focus on insight and innovation. **Dynamics** meetings are about reflection and relationships. Here's a table showing the area of focus for each of the three Ds.

Direction	Discovery	Dynamics
Sharing business context	Increasing visibility of what each participant in a project is working on	Celebrating success
Solving problems or testing early thinking	Generating new ideas	Debriefing failures and talking about learnings
Making decisions	Bringing in external data and perspectives	Reviewing stakeholder engagement and planning
Identifying and working through opportunities for improvement	Sharing information that affects others	Checking in on team behaviours

FIGURE 12 The 3 Ds of Meetings

With a better understanding of the importance of purpose in meeting, you can get down to the nitty gritty: things like the agenda, how often to meet, the length of meetings, who needs to attend, and so forth. This nitty gritty detail is like choosing flooring—it's got to be fit for purpose. No one puts wool carpet in their workshed, so make sure your meetings are also fit for purpose.

The 3Ds are like the blueprint or plans for your renovation—they tell you where to start and how to proceed. And just like well laid plans, sometimes they have to be modified as you get into the work. One meeting might have a bit of discovery, a bit of dynamics and a bit of direction. That's fine. The key is clarity. Just as you wouldn't renovate a house without a plan and budget, you shouldn't go into your meeting without a clear intention. As long as your meetings have a clear purpose and focus, your team will be banging down the door of your physical and virtual meeting rooms, knowing that meetings in your organisation are all about energising the team and feeling good because they move the work forward. They make the work work for everyone, and they are one more small step towards excellence.

QUICK, QUALITY CHATS

Quick chat, big impact:
Even a short, sincere chat can enhance
connection and wellbeing.

DO YOU have a spare forty-five seconds? No? Never mind, move on to the next practice. If you do have forty-five seconds to spare, you have more than enough time to have a quick chat, but I'm not talking about small talk here. If you have the skill and awareness, you can turn a quick chat into a high-impact interaction. It can happen in the blink of an eye; an elevator ride is enough time. I know, because it happened to me.

I was standing in an elevator one day when the doors swished open and in stepped the CEO. Three seconds and three words later, I was in tears.

The three words were 'How are you?' My answer, if I'd managed to get it out before the lump rose in my throat, would have been, 'So bad.' Because I wasn't doing well. I had frustration and stress coming at me from my 'home team'. I was worried about project deadlines and the risks involved if I missed them. Plus I had some troubling news on the home front. We all know what it's like to be in a bad place emotionally. And usually we manage to keep our upper lips stiff enough for no one to notice. The difference that day in the lift—the reason my lip trembled and gave way—was the sincerity, warmth, and genuine focused presence that the CEO embodied. His question wasn't a formality, it was an authentic enquiry and he cared about the answer. I'd been flying through the front doors day after day, chirping a cheery 'Fine, thanks' when the receptionist gave me her standard, 'Hi Louise, how are you?' But when the CEO turned to me, gave me his full attention and spoke the same words, I was undone. The façade fell away, my vulnerability took centre stage, and I experienced a moment of genuine connection as the CEO held space for me. It was the quickest of chats, but I had just experienced a high-impact interaction.

Now, I'm not for a moment suggesting you start ambushing your team members in the lift and trying to make them cry, but this little anecdote does a good job of showing how powerful high-impact interactions in the form of a quick chat can be. Those conversations can be upbeat, downbeat or somewhere in the middle. They're definitely not 'small talk', but they're not necessarily 'deep and meaningful' either, although they can be. Potential topics are myriad. The purposes are varied. These conversations can be formal or informal. They can happen in both good times and bad. You don't need to have deep personal knowledge of the person you're chatting with. You don't need to have spent a lot of time with them. And you don't have to have all the answers. My CEO did *not* begin a therapy session between the third and thirteenth floor! Just knowing someone genuinely cared was enough to uplift me.

In her work on high-quality connections, researcher Jane Dutton identified that even short, quick chats can become high-impact interactions. She also found that contemporary society has become increasingly characterised by temporary connections and swift coordination. This is particularly true of the workplace. Hybrid working has contributed to this. Many people are telling me that when they're working from home, the only time they talk to people is in meetings. Or during a couple of minutes before the meeting kicks off when people make awkward small talk. All this means high-quality connections must be built quickly and across organisational boundaries. Quick chats that create a high-impact interaction are crucial for leaders who want to develop individuals and build strong organisations.[18]

---

18 Dutton, Jane, John Paul Stephens, & Emily Heaphy. *High Quality Connections*. White Paper. Centre for Positive Organizations.

These types of interactions with your team have many benefits. And yes, conversations that leave people in tears can be beneficial. Most of us know that a good cry gives us a release. It's good for our wellbeing. Quality conversations help us feel good and do well. They help us build relationships at work. When we have a work 'best friend' we're more engaged. The working day has small pleasures that we look forward to. It's like a sunflower leaning towards the sun. The warmth and light uplifts us. We savour the positive feelings these moments create. Any type of contact is potentially high-quality, and just one moment of quality connection can leave a spring in your step and create ripples that spread out across a team. Research tells us that it takes just one micro-moment of genuine connection to spark that upward spiral of mutual care between people.[19] During that brief exchange, we mirror each other's body and brain activity and our impulse to care for each other. This is known as 'positive resonance'.

Have you ever been for a morning swim in the sea in winter? Perhaps taken an ice bath or even just a cold shower? Maybe you think people who do that are crazy, but there's a reason for it—afterwards they feel a rush of warmth. The 'post-swim high', or 'cold-water euphoria', has been well documented. The swimmer or bather is invigorated by a rush of endorphins, the body's natural feel-good chemicals

---

19 Dutton, Jane. *Energize Your Workplace: How to Create and Sustain High-Quality Connections at Work.* Jossey-Bass. 2003.

that stimulate circulation and boost mood. The positive resonance people feel after a positive, high-impact interaction in the form of a quick chat is like that warmth that spreads through the swimmer's body when they emerge from the cold water. It creates a feeling of vitality that enhances the wellbeing of each individual. It fortifies us and helps to build up our psychological and emotional resources. It's the perfect antidote to loneliness and other experiences that drain our energy every day. And when every individual feels that rush of warmth, the whole team starts to feel good.

Making it work

It would be nice if I could give you a script here, and in a minute we'll go a bit deeper into how to have a quick chat that creates a high-impact interaction, but the words in a script are less important than the way you deliver them. If you're swiping or typing on your phone while you talk to somebody, it's pretty clear you'd rather be somewhere else. Eye contact is recommended if that's in the comfort zone for both of you. Facing the person is essential. Don't give them the cold shoulder. A lot of this is body language 101, but it's important not be mechanical about it. Adjusting the way you're standing, thinking about your expression and keeping your hands away from your phone or keyboard are reminders to go deeper and find an authentic place to start. If your mind and heart are sincere, your body language will be too. Find that place, focus your attention and ask appreciative questions. That is how to make your connection with others count. It sounds simple, but simple doesn't mean easy.

Developing better connections at work can be done in many ways. As well as engaging respectfully with others by being present when you talk to them, make sure you listen actively, ask questions, affirm their thoughts and feelings and share information with them. If they tell you about their fishing trip on the weekend, don't nod politely as your eyes glaze over; offer something in return. Invest time in your friendships and celebrate the positive things, no matter how small.

You can also try popping reminders in your diary to check in with certain team members—perhaps ones you don't often see when you walk the floor. And remember to do that floor walk occasionally— be present and available and create opportunities for high-impact interactions. Make sure that you pop on your 'positive specs' every now and then. Keeping your eyes peeled for the positives in others is a great way of creating micro-moments of connection. Look through those lenses for the times when your colleagues' strengths are on display. Then, once you have a spare moment, let them know what you noticed and why using those strengths is valuable.

High-impact interactions lead to high-quality connections. When your team is connected in this way, the wellbeing of the whole group is uplifted.

Everybody starts to feel good. It helps us feel more grateful, more optimistic and more positive about our future. We feel a greater sense of belonging. We're more likely to feel psychologically safe and bring our authentic voice to work without fear of rejection. If we consistently make moments (or micromoments) count, they'll make a considerable difference to our wellbeing and the wellbeing of those around us. Improved wellbeing means the work starts to work for everyone, and moves the team towards excellence.

TEAM GROWTH

GIVE (GOOD) FEEDBACK; GET (GOOD) FEEDBACK

Clean feedback, clear growth: Use the Four Cs—
Clean, Clear, Contextual and Circular—to give feed-
back that's effective, fair and helps everyone grow.

THERE ARE topics I pondered whether to include in this book because they're what I call 'eye-rollers'— dull, over-exposed and often outdated subjects that cause a sudden surge in sick leave when they're on a meeting agenda. Feedback isn't outdated, but neither is it something new. It's like the 'eat vegetables and exercise to stay healthy' advice that we have all absorbed. It's business 101. I know you know you need to give it. And maybe you are. But there's a fair chance you're not. And if you are giving it, it can always be fine-tuned.

Feedback is inevitable. We all receive it, and we're all affected by it. Feedback is everywhere and takes many forms. It can be written or verbal, and delivered as data or behaviour. If you rolled your eyes when you read the word 'Feedback' at the top of this page, that would have been feedback for me... if I'd been a fly on the wall. It would also have been feedback to yourself about what you think about feedback. Like I said: it's everywhere. But is it helping your team to get better?

Have you ever stopped to ask yourself: is the feedback you're giving and receiving *good* feedback? I'm not talking about the content of feedback. That can't always be 'good'. If it was always positive, always took the form of praise, there would be no growth. When I say 'good' feedback, I'm talking about its structure and impact being effective and helpful.

Good feedback fuels our growth. It moves a team forward, not backward. It's the starting point for a curious conversation to help us lead and perform to bring out our best. Good feedback is used as a learning and discovery tool, not an opportunity for a lecture or a dressing down. Feedback is not a weapon.

Good feedback ignites change and helps us get moving and experimenting with new ways of doing things. But it also tells us whether we're on the right track and allows us to course-correct if we're heading in the wrong direction. It's the guard rails in a ten-pin bowling alley that prevent the ball from skidding across the room and knocking someone off their feet. Without feedback, we're flying blind and missing opportunities.

Now let's go a little deeper.

Good feedback must be delivered safely, because 'unsafe' feedback can backfire badly. In one study, a whopping eighty-three per cent of employees reported that negative feedback decreased their ability to perform better.[20] Another study found that receivers' heart rates jumped enough to indicate moderate or extreme duress in unprompted feedback situations. Research has shown that simply hearing the word 'feedback' can be triggering.[21] Feedback represents social threats concerning status and anxiety, and our brains' threat response can be triggered in the face of these threats in the same way it is when facing physical danger.[22] And it's not just negative feedback that can be dangerous; endless rounds of positive feedback can result in diminishing returns. I experienced that myself when multiple rounds of feedback on a paper I was working on felt more like anxiety-fuelled perfectionism than essential corrections. Not having a clear cut-off point for feedback can also be anxiety-inducing—something else I have experienced personally.

So before delivering feedback, ask yourself a few questions. Has the recipient given consent? Will it trigger them? Think about this: feedback

---

20 Guo, Y., Zhang, Y., Liao, J., Guo, X., Liu, J., Xue, X.,... Zhang, Y. (2017). Negative Feedback And Employee Job Performance: Moderating Role Of The Big Five. *Social Behavior and Personality*, 45(10), 1735-1744. doi:https:// doi.org/10.2224/sbp.6478

21 https://www.strategy-business.com/article/ Using-Neuroscience-to-Make-Feedback-Work-and-Feel-Better

22 For more detailed insights, refer to David Rock's work, including his articles and the *SCARF: A Brain-Based Model for Collaborating with and Influencing Others*, which discusses these social threats in detail.

has elements of assessment and appraisal, but to the recipient this can feel like criticism. And while nobody actually likes being criticised, for some people it can be traumatising. Do you know everything about the recipient's past or personal life? Trauma is widespread in society, but often invisible. What wound could your feedback inadvertently open?

Rejection sensitivity is something else to beware of. This is a very real issue, which can be common among ADHDers and other groups. People with unrelenting standards of perfectionism can feel utterly crippled by negative feedback, however constructive it is. If you want to give them feedback that propels them forward, you will have to do it right. If it's not done safely and with care, it can backfire and there can be flow-on impacts and repercussions.

I know you want to make the experience of giving and receiving feedback a positive one. One that not only feels good for everyone involved, but makes a real difference in people's lives and helps your team to get better. Research has found that roughly eighty-seven per cent of employees want to 'be developed' in their job. And how many of them report receiving the feedback they need to do that? Only one third.[23] So what are the characteristics of feedback that is fit for purpose?

Good feedback must be clean. No, I don't mean put it in the washing machine. I mean make sure it's not stained with bias or sullied by a hidden agenda.

---

23 https://www.strategy-business.com/article/Using-Neuroscience-to-Make-Feedback-Work-and-Feel-Better

I know what it's like to receive 'dirty' feedback. I recall a casual conversation I had with a manager years ago. She told me that I went from thought to action very quickly. That there wasn't a lot of reflection time in my thinking processes and decision-making. The feedback was that I shouldn't do that; I should slow down. I took the feedback on board, but it didn't sit well and gave me a queasy feeling when I thought about it. Fortunately my orientation to action had no negative impact, and I was recognised as a high performer in the company. It was only years later that I realised the feedback I'd received was not based on any observation, data or facts, and was also just plain wrong. The high level of initiation in my behaviour was an important characteristic for working with start-ups and entrepreneurs. What I had been told was a weakness was actually a critical strength for the context I was working in. So why was I given feedback that was so obviously wrong? Why would someone give me bad advice? Is it possible that jealousy or envy was informing the feedback? I have no idea; it's possible. It's also possible my manager was projecting her way of working onto me. I send that manager good vibes today and thank her for a lesson learnt, which is that this stuff happens, but it wastes time you could be using to deliver for your team and customers.

Good feedback is about the receiver, not the giver. Too often it reflects the bias or insecurities of the senior person giving it; make sure the feedback you give is not about yourself and your personal limitations.

Feedback should have a goal and address specific issues. It is not an opportunity for a whinge session or a forum for complaints. Be clear in what you say. Beating around the bush and talking in riddles is not helpful. In fact it's cruel. Good feedback is constructive; if it's not constructive, it's not feedback. And if it's not clear, it's not constructive.

Feedback must also be contextual and appropriate for the specific work situation. For example, let's say your marketing team has multiple projects running at once. But resources are stretched and little mistakes are creeping into the work. The internal presentation decks have typos and the design of the planning documents is a little rough. But the campaigns are creating a lot of excitement in the company and everybody is energised by the projects. So is it useful feedback to point out typos the team knows are there, and are only there because resources are stretched? No, that feedback doesn't consider the context and sounds like nitpicking and micromanaging.

Good feedback is reciprocal and should open a two-way conversation. It's not a lecture. If typos are sneaking into internal documents, the marketing team need to give their managers feedback that they need more resources to make those documents perfect. The person giving feedback should also have the appropriate authority. The head of finance shouldn't tell the head of marketing how to do their job, and the head of marketing probably shouldn't give the head of finance tips on profit forecasting.

Making it work

Feedback is a huge topic. I could talk about it all day. I could talk all day about the models and techniques created to help administer it. Models like SBI—situation, behaviour, impact—which I'm sure you've heard of. But here I'd like to share a more principled approach—one you may not have heard of and one that I've developed that's a bit different. I call it the Four Cs, and it brings together everything I've been talking about here. It's also contemporary. Now, more than ever, I work with organisations that have a high number of neurodivergent people in their workforce. The world of work is not yet well designed for people with these brain types; I should know, I'm one of them. It's important that *everyone* receives good, clean feedback.

The beauty of the Four Cs principles is that they clearly define the gold standard of feedback, and you can use them as a quick reference before giving feedback to ensure a good experience for both giver and receiver. As I said earlier, feedback is about the giver and the receiver. Applying the Four Cs ensures a growth experience for both. The self-reflection involved in cleaning the feedback, and the circular nature create opportunities for both people to learn and grow in their understanding.

Let's have a look at the principles...

CLEAN. Self-reflection must take place and you must consider your intent before giving feedback. Ask yourself why you're providing this feedback now. What does it say about you and your possible limitations? How might you be wrong? There are things we generally take as fact, but when we clean them we find they're subject to bias and potentially neuronormative standards. Here are some examples:

- The person leaves things to the last minute (some people do their best work with an elongated incubation period)

- The person is abrupt (some people are direct communicators)

- The person is not concentrating or showing interest as they're looking away (eye contact can reduce some people's ability to concentrate)

- The person is unhappy (not everyone smiles to show they're happy)

- The person prefers not to take phone calls (asynchronous comms like email or voice notes is a valid way of talking and allows for the processing time some people need and value)

To make sure you really nail this important C, here's a checklist:

- What have I observed objectively? What's the impact?

- What do I know and what don't I know?

- What assumptions might I be making?

- What assumptions might the recipient be holding?

- What story could I be making up?

- What is this situation or person activating in me?

- How can I learn from this?

- How can I start this 'feedback' conversation in a safe and productive way?

CLEAR. There is a myth that feedback has to be delivered as a 'sandwich'—that criticism should be the filling between two slices of positivity. Not necessarily. As Brené Brown said, 'Clear is kind.' As much as possible be specific, direct and timely, and explain the impact.

CONTEXTUAL. Consider the feedback in context. How is the environment or the 'system' affecting the behaviour or other issues you're discussing?

CIRCULAR. When giving feedback ask questions, check for understanding and allow the recipient to provide their own input. Feedback should be a dialogue.

Feedback can feel tough, but it doesn't have to be. If you want to do feedback well, you must learn to administer it safely—in the right form, in the right dose and at the right time. Even though we might know, cognitively, that 'feedback is a gift' or 'feedback is the breakfast of champions', it's hard. Often because we've previously had a bad experience with feedback. If that's the case, I suggest a reframe. Don't call it feedback. It's just a conversation to

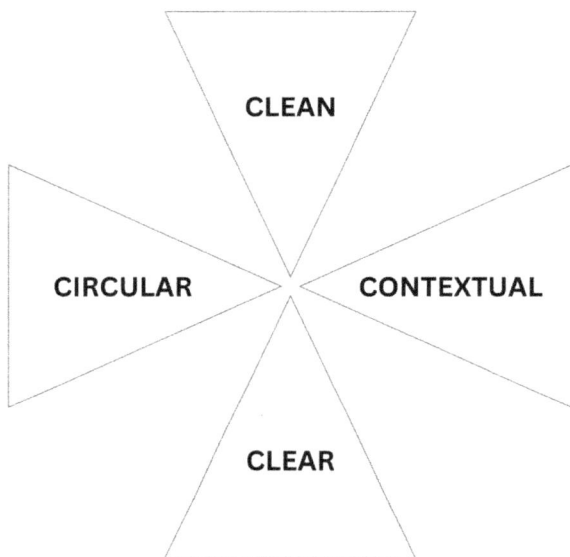

FIGURE 13 The 4 Cs of Feedback

create change. Also remember to go for progress over perfection. 'Done' is better than 'perfect'. That applies in terms of the results you want to see from the feedback you give, but also in the way you deliver feedback. But by using the Four Cs, your skill in giving feedback—that is, having conversations that create change—will also progress.

Improving your skills in giving and receiving feedback is like a little burst on the growth pedal. When your team welcomes feedback instead of fearing it, work starts to work and the whole team takes a step towards excellence.

LEARN TOGETHER; GROW TOGETHER

Harder, better, faster, stronger: Don't just grow a group of individuals, Grow your team.

HAVE YOU ever played basketball? Or netball or football or cricket or any other team sport? My son was about seven years old when his basketball team competed in their first season. As you can imagine, little boys need a bit of practice and training before they can join the Harlem Globetrotters! The littlies were all at very different stages of development when it came to their individual skills. Some had to work on their dribbling, others focused on passing and not hogging the ball, and still others were spending time on shooting goals. But here's the thing—they were also working on their team skills. Together, they focused on practising rebounds and getting the ball back down their side of the court. That's what they went over in group training each week. And that's what helped the team grow as a team. A team that learns together, grows together. A team that grows together is getting better all the time.

Workplace teams are not that different from sports teams. Individual members will have development plans, but teams at the edge of excellence also have team growth goals and a plan to get there. When a leader develops—grows—their team *as* a team, the team will not only deliver their part of the organisational strategy but the team experience will be enhanced. And everybody will want to be on that team.

We all know what it's like to be on an awesome team. A team that's firing on all cylinders and hitting the bullseye every time. One where individual members do more than pull their weight—they go above and beyond for the sake of the team. It's about more than getting prompt answers to questions—it's about anticipating each other's needs as if you were psychic. It's about more than job satisfaction—it's about believing in the mission. And it's also about more than skills, knowledge and experience. It's about the vibe—how it feels to be on the team. And being on a team like that feels amazing.

Companies spend a lot of time analysing data and trying to improve their customer experience, but not many are giving the same attention to their team experience. A team is home base for its members. Being in a team should feel like coming home. It's an anchor that provides stability when you're floating around within the larger organisation. A team has a certain vibe, and that vibe has to be right for everyone. People need to feel like they belong. And they want to feel like they belong to a winning team. They want to come to work and feel uplifted.

That 'winning feeling' develops over time, and that development should be deliberate. The team experience should be co-created by the team itself; it's not a top-down activity but is co-designed by the team and for the team. And everybody should be held accountable—people need to care about this. Creating the team experience should be guided by what people want for and from their team. This helps the team to grow. Momentum creates a good experience, which in turn fuels more growth. When the team experience is good, you can do anything.

But the key to an amazing team experience might surprise you. Like I said before, it's not just a sum of the individuals in that team. It's about learning. And growing. And learning and growing together. We can think about goals here, specifically learning goals. But I'm not talking about personal goals or anything written in somebody's performance review or individual development plan. Those plans relate to growing in a role and performing, and perhaps even consider an overall career. Everyone has these 'me-goals'. You might have a team purpose and roadmap, too. There is also the broader organisational plan or strategy. But there's something missing in between these things. How might the team learn and grow *as a team*? In other words, what are the team's 'we-goals'? We-goals do not replace me-goals or organisational goals. We-goals define what the focus is when it comes to learning and team growth. How can the team mature? For my son's basketball team, the dribbling and goal-shooting practice were me-goals, while the rebound practice they did at training sessions was a we-goal.

When you have a plan for your team experience, how it's going to be created and how your team will grow, all of these things stack up and link. But in my experience, that plan is often missing. Teams that work intentionally to grow together and embrace continuous learning are stronger. When this team growth is layered on top of individual growth, the whole structure is reinforced and becomes stronger than the sum of its parts. Resilience is a byproduct. The team's full potential is realised, and no money is left on the table. Everyone is on the same page and pulling in the same direction. Unlike the previous sentences, there is internal consistency and alignment and no one is mixing metaphors.

Again, this is not about output. A strong, resilient team that embraces a learning culture will surely perform better, but it goes further. The team becomes more responsive to the market, the capacity for dealing with uncertainty is built up. A tight, synchronised unit makes a superb project team. Like a commando unit parachuting into a trouble spot, a multidisciplinary team can be dropped into other areas of an organisation and deployed for an effective, efficient, laser-focused mission.

Like I said, not a lot of companies have an intentional focus on co-creating their team experience. Sure, there's a lot of team bonding activities around with a focus on connection. But what's missing is how the team needs to learn and grow—together. It's this learning that creates that special, elusive 'vibe' that makes everybody want to be on that team. Moving beyond mere connection and making this intentional will give you an edge. This is about consciously creating a culture of continuous learning and growth to get your team buzzing with an electrifying vibe.

Making it work

You might want to bring in a professional to help you with this, but if you want to try a DIY version, set aside some time to start this conversation as a team. Make sure you have the organisational strategy plan and purpose, plus your business unit/team strategy or OKRs in place first. Also make sure you explain why you're doing this and what the benefits are. Remember: this is a proactive exercise that's about the growth of the team. It's not an exercise to work out who's being exited or replaced! (If that's your intention, please don't do this exercise.)

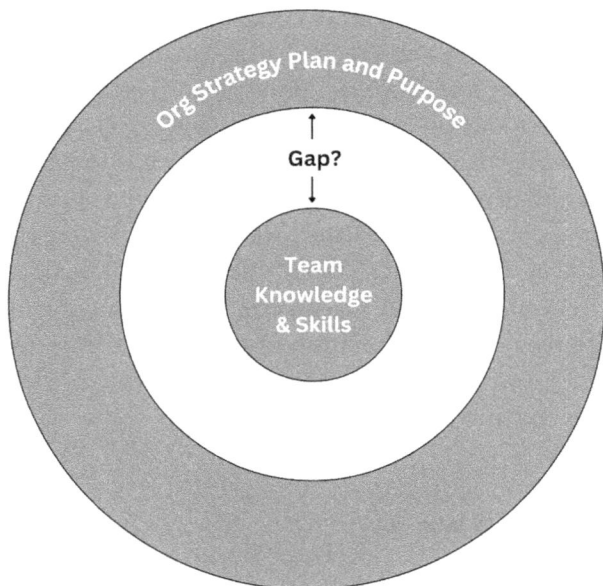

FIGURE 14 The Skills/Knowledge Gap

Now, open the discussion with the following questions:

1 Given the broader organisational strategy plan and purpose, what knowledge, skills and capabilities does our team need so we can deliver our purpose?

2 As a team, how do we rate our current level of knowledge, skills and capabilities? Do we have what we need to deliver our purpose?

3 What's the gap?

4 How might we close the gap? What do we need to learn, individually and as a team?

5   How do we need the process of learning and
    growth to unfold as a team?

For example, you might find that you have a team of subject matter experts who are passionate about their field and have great depth of expertise but lack the capacity to manage, plan and execute change projects. The change initiative could be about anything—say, trying to reduce domestic violence in the community. If the team lacks project management skills required to move the work forward, the work won't—well—move forward. Benefits could be left on the table. Significant and important benefits. This can be addressed through a range of interventions such as mentoring, team coaching, facilitation and training. Through this work, the team grows, and through that growth the team experience is changed for the better.

When working through the process above, don't neglect Step 5. Everyone needs to be on the same page from the get-go. They need to know what they're signing up to. You need to embed deliberate practices into the way things are done. Look at rituals and behaviours that create structured spaces in which to reflect and learn. These can be unconventional practices like muck-up moments or f*** up nights. Or they can be more refined. At one organisation I worked with, the kick-off phase of a project typically included agreement on the 'project team sliders'. The sliders represented variables to consider, such as pace, and the team would agree whether that slider was on or off and how high it would be. It doesn't matter what you use, as long as it works. And remember, the approach will be different for every team.

To achieve more, a team has to *be* more. When a team *is* more, then the team experience feels amazing. The team can do anything. Weaker members will be strengthened by continuous learning. Instead of operating at the level of the lowest common denominator, the whole team will rise to new heights. When we think about what a team can achieve, Aristotle had it right –'The whole is greater than the sum of its parts.'

When a team learns together, it grows together. It gets better. Work starts to work for everybody, and the whole team takes one more step towards excellence.

NOTICE THE NOISE; FIND THE NEED[57]

Notice the noise, find the need: Find the real need behind workplace noise to drive team growth.

LET'S SAY you're at your desk one morning, deep in thought and trying to solve a tricky problem. Your focus is intense and the world seems far away. Then your concentration is shattered when a high-pitched scream echoes through the open-plan office. You look up from your desk and see that everyone is on their feet and craning their necks to see which desk the screeching is coming from. Obviously, you have to investigate. You sigh, close your laptop, and steel yourself as you walk towards the noise to find

---

24 I wish to acknowledge the following people for helping me to understand the concept of noise versus need: my colleague Paul Zonneveld, author of *Emergent: the power of systemic intelligence to navigate the complexity of M&A*, David Whyte and his powerful poems, and Joan Lurie, CEO of Orgonomics.

out what's wrong. But is the noise really the source of the trouble?

Of course, I'm sure that high-pitched screaming is NOT part of the daily entertainment in your workplace. But I'm also sure that there is plenty of 'noise' whenever a problem crops up, and that your instinct, when things get noisy, is to follow that noise and silence it. It's like when your burglar alarm goes off; all you can think about is killing that ear-piercing, neighbourhood-waking din. But is that the right approach, or is it a bit like treating symptoms to cure a disease? When an alarm goes off at 2:00 am, if you don't investigate further it may well go off again at 3:00 am. Has there been a security breach? Is there a glitch in the system? Maybe the system was never installed properly and has to be re-installed. Treating symptoms doesn't work, because to cure the disease you have to find the root cause.

To find the unmet need that is causing a problem, sometimes we have to scratch and sniff. What's really going on? What is the elephant in the room? Employment engagement surveys are a classic way of identifying issues, but they don't necessarily identify needs. For example, say the team points to a communication problem. Sounds easy to fix— instigate an open-door policy, send out a weekly newsletter, walk the floor and say good morning to everyone. And sure, such tactics might result in *more* communication, but won't necessarily be *better* communication. Assumptions often get in the way here. Perhaps team members are keeping quiet and not speaking up about issues or challenges in order to maintain a harmonious atmosphere. They don't want conflict. The need here is not more communication, but permission to raise issues without fear. Your team won't grow—won't get better—unless you fix the underlying causes of an issue.

Consider the matter of workforce participation by women. Years ago I was approached by a STEM company that was haemorrhaging women. The management had the bright idea that running an International Women's Day Rev-Up (featuring cupcakes, no less) would solve the problem. They asked me to appear as the keynote speaker. I said no to this one-hour engagement as they didn't have anything planned afterwards to address their big hairy challenge. It was obvious to me that cupcakes were not the answer, and no matter how much I inspire change in my keynote, I wasn't prepared to do it if they weren't going to commit to follow-up activity that would create real change. And that was regardless of whether that follow-up activity included me. Women were leaving—that was the noise. But they didn't need cupcakes or a keynote; they needed systemic change—that was the need. The upshot was that I was engaged for a longer-term project that did just that.

These are just a couple of examples of how the noise in a workplace might be hiding the real need and stunting the growth of your teams. There are many ways in which a workplace can be 'noisy', for example:

- People are focused on their own agendas.

- There's conflict with stakeholders and people are ignoring them.

- Everyone avoids stepping into each other's turf.

- People keep knowledge and expertise to themselves.

- Stakeholders don't really know what you stand for.

- There's duplication and a lot of wasted effort and time.

- You don't recognise or address issues with quality.

- Learning is focused only on individuals, not the team.

- Innovation is slow, and there's resistance to change.

- You hear things like 'we need a seat at the table' and 'we work in siloes' and 'we haven't had a team-building day in a while...

And so on and so on. I know these are common issues because when leaders get in touch and ask me to come in and work their teams and provide training, about eighty per cent of the time they ask for a solution based on the noise.

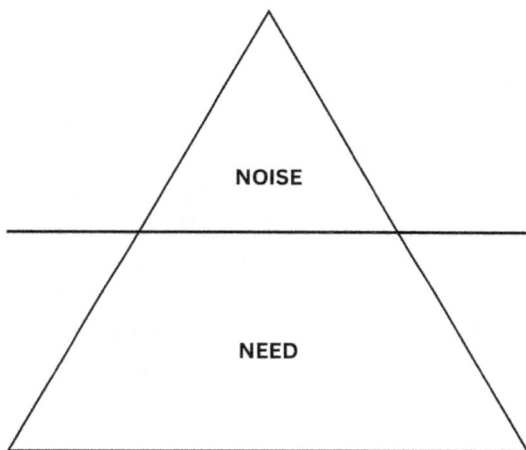

FIGURE 15 Need or Noise?

This topic is important. If you have unaddressed needs, problems will re-appear. The employee engagement survey will say exactly the same thing the following year. Without understanding the real need, the team cannot grow and may even begin to deteriorate. You might find yourself desperately throwing money and resources at more and more training, only to find the time and effort is wasted because it was aimed at the wrong target. But by following the need, not the noise, you will identify exactly where to place your resources. It's like finding the acupressure point to cure a headache. It's not anywhere in your head, as you might expect, but in the webbing between your thumb and index finger.

Making it work

Let's say there's some noise you've tuned into or has been blasted your way. You have to do something—now! But the danger here is that you lean into short-term solutions just to keep things quiet. You might even be doing that without realising it. (It's okay to be honest—we're just having a private chat within the pages of this book.) If all you do is silence the noise, it will crop up again later because you haven't filled the needs creating the noise. When this happens, any hope of achieving longer-term benefits are handcuffed.

This happens a lot. And I get how difficult it can be. You want to keep the peace. To keep everybody happy, you need to demonstrate that something has been done. But try to be aware of when you're leaning into these Band-Aid solutions. If you are, perhaps start with the quick fix but know that it's just that, and use it to inspire change that drives longer-term, transformational growth. Perhaps the problem or the challenge can't fully be defined. In which case, that's the starting point; be curious, speak to people on your team to understand what's playing out. The important thing is to know what you're doing—are you following the noise or the need?

I've had years of experience with inspiring change and creating real shifts and transformational outcomes, but writing out some guidance on how you, the reader, could identify whether you're following the need or the noise was tricky. On one hand, I know my readers value practical guidance, but on the other hand, one size doesn't fit all with this practice—especially without knowing your context. But I can at least get you started. So here's an idea...

Take a moment to close the door or find some private space. Try to clear your mind. Now get out a sheet of paper, draw a triangle on it, and draw a line through the middle of the triangle, like the figure above. In the top half of the triangle, I want you to try to write down what the noise is. You don't necessarily have to use words. You can draw a picture if you want. In the bottom half of the triangle, write down the unaddressed needs you think are creating this noise. Again, you can express yourself in pictures if that feels right. Then, if you can think of a solution, write it underneath the triangle. Don't worry if you can't think of a solution. You may need some external help with this.

Now sit back in your chair and look at the paper. Does it all make sense? Are you able to identify what the noise is compared to the need? Is the solution you have in mind a cure or just a Band-Aid? Don't be afraid to admit to yourself that you may have got it wrong. It's just you and the piece of paper and maybe a cappuccino if you've headed to a local café to do this exercise. As I said, it's hard to 'do the needful'. Identifying what's noise, working out what the need is and translating that into a solution is contextual and not straightforward. This is when you might benefit from bringing in an expert in change and leaders often come to me for this.

Like I said, this topic is highly contextual, and I can't prescribe a cure-all for your problems. But I can encourage you to deliberately think about these issues. To be intentional and honest with yourself. This is important for team growth. When voices are raised in frustration or anger, when gossip and complaints fill the airwaves, progress is impossible. Listen to the noise but follow the trail until you find the need. This press on the growth pedal may be just what you need for your team to get better and feel like work is working for them.

TEAM
PERFORMANCE

ALIGNED
PURPOSE

*Aligned purpose, aligned efforts: Create
a team purpose that everyone can get
behind and boost team performance.*

WHEN I WORK with teams to boost their performance,
I often ask, 'What's the team there for?' This is usually
followed by several seconds of silence, followed by
the question, 'What do you mean?' There's a frown,
sometimes a laugh, and then they say, 'Oh that's
obvious.' But their reply doesn't quite answer the
question. Then a light bulb goes on and they say,
'Hang on a minute, let me look it up in my deck...'
Another several-second delay while they click their
mouse a few times, followed by, 'Oh, here it is!' And
they read out the company purpose, verbatim, from
their laptop.

Something else I like to do is ask workshop participants to write down their team purpose on a

piece of paper. They do this separately and anonymously and I make it clear that this is not a test, but nevertheless, a mixture of giggles and red faces ensue when I read the purpose(s) out and discover no two are the same. Most leaders believe everyone in their team knows what the team is there to do. But in my experience, they're rarely aligned. Having a statement—a few words on paper—is helpful, but it's the process of reflecting and sharing what everybody is there to do that really engages and energises the team. It's not the statement, but the conversations about that statement that connects and aligns the team.

Team purpose is the fundamental reason for a team's existence. It serves as a guiding principle that aligns team members' efforts, actions and decisions towards a common goal. It has three elements:

- What your team does or delivers,
- Who you do it for, and
- Why you do it.

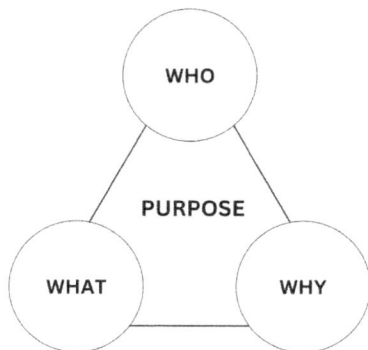

FIGURE 16 Aligned Purpose

Team purpose also has to feed into and enable the organisation's purpose. I've worked with many organisations that say there is only one purpose, and that's the organisation's purpose. That's fine, I get it, but in my opinion, it's just semantics. A team is like an army regiment. The overall purpose of the army is to win the war, but the regiment has an operational objective that is aligned with and serves that greater purpose in a specific way. Whether your team purpose is the same as the organisation's purpose, or something more specific, you must be on the same page and clear about how what you do contributes to the bigger picture.

For example, the purpose of the operations team at Amazon is to streamline the supply chain, ensure timely deliveries and enhance customer satisfaction by optimising logistics. This supports the broader organisational purpose to 'be the Earth's most customer-centric company.'

Team purpose does not necessarily have to be a 'higher' purpose. It can and should be if that is the space your organisation operates in, but a more important factor when it comes to team purpose is that it is *aligned*. Everybody must know what it is and have that purpose at the heart of what they do. Team purpose must be clearly articulated and consistently reinforced, but it must also be more than just words on a document. It should be at the heart of every decision and action that a team makes or undertakes. Amazon's purpose shapes all the company's strategies and decisions, ensuring that the customer is always the focal point.

An aligned purpose is clear, provides stable, unchanging goals, is communicated effectively, and serves to unite a team. When a team's purpose is aligned, everybody is rowing in the same direction. A clear purpose acts as a north star, fostering unity and synergy within the team. To build a high-performing team, agreement on the mission is crucial. People want to understand the 'why' behind their actions because they crave a sense of direction and meaning. There's a reason Simon Sinek's TED talk, 'Start with Why', has been watched 27 million times (and undoubtedly more, at the time you're reading this).

If your team purpose is out of alignment, take cover, because arrows will come flying from all directions. Without guiding principles, decisions become impossible. When stakeholders are unsure of what the team stands for, they may confuse their purpose with creating a product—possibly a useless and expensive one. Individuals will be off chasing their own agendas, wasting resources and effort. The company will exist to serve individual growth over collaborative growth—employees will be there to make a s*** load of money. The leader's desk will be collapsing under a growing pile of problems, dumped there by disgruntled team members who have made no effort to initiate a solution.

When faced with seemingly intractable problems in your team, realigning the purpose may be the antidote. It's like cutting the Gordian knot—applying a simple and direct approach to a deceptively complex problem. Bringing your team into alignment may have surprising, unexpected and far-reaching effects that take the heat out of multiple problems. Having this clear sense of what a team is there to do is really energising and motivating. When I work with teams to revisit that, we often see a life in engagement. It can reinvigorate the team.

Making it work

Creating a team purpose is a fairly simple process and can help discover where the misalignment is. For example, some people on a team might think their purpose is to *support* an initiative, while others think their purpose is to *drive* that initiative. Orientation can also be misaligned, with team members feeling strongly that they serve completely different groups of people. When the misalignment is revealed, it's possible to realign the team purpose. As I said, it's simple, but it's not easy. There's nuance; there's subtlety.

The process must also be a group activity. You don't want purpose to be handed to people, and you certainly don't want to shove it down their throats and tell them to swallow. That's more likely to make them gag. As one leader I know said, after leaving an organisation where she was force-fed the company's purpose, 'I've had to detox from the purpose that was "given" to me.' Purpose must be co-created; it has to 'taste' good.

I've broken this process down into five steps. Allocate forty-five minutes for the following activity, which can be done in-person, virtually or hybrid.

1 **Bring your team together**

- Tell the team that you've brought them together to create an aligned team purpose.

- Explain that there's nothing heavy going on here—you simply want to make sure you're all 'rowing in the same direction'.

- Tell them not to worry about perfection in this exercise—eighty per cent done is good enough.

2 **Break into groups**

- Divide the team into groups of two or three.

- Ask each group to work together to create a draft purpose statement.

3 **Ask the following questions to guide your group's thinking**

- What does your team do or deliver?

- Who do you do it for?

- Why do you do it?

4 **Ask your team to pitch their purpose statement**

- Each group pitches their purpose statement to the entire team.

- Encourage open discussions.

5   **Create a cohesive purpose statement**

- Merge the best elements from each statement to form a purpose that reflects the teams' aspirations.

- **TIPS**: Don't waffle. Keep your statement short so it's energising. Make it descriptive enough so it's practical. Use simple language.

Once you have your team purpose statement wrapped up, put it into action. It can guide many aspects of your team's performance, such as:

- **Goals and success measures**: Align your goals with your purpose and define how you will measure success.

- **Priorities**: Prioritise actions that support your purpose.

- **Roles and KPIs**: Evaluate roles and key performance indicators to ensure they support the refined purpose.

- **Decision-making**: Establish decision-making criteria that align with your purpose and integrate your purpose into the decision-making process.

- **Meeting agendas**: Conducting team meetings with your purpose in mind will ensure the right discussions and information sharing.

- **Stakeholder engagement**: Communicating your purpose clearly to stakeholders will foster mutual understanding.

When team purpose is aligned, problems are minimised. If issues are coming at you from all directions and solutions seem elusive, take some time to ensure your team purpose is aligned. It may just be the quick press on that performance pedal you need to create ongoing peace and productivity. Work starts to work for everyone. The team moves closer to the edge of excellence.

GREAT RELATIONSHIPS

Great relationships, great teams: Strong bonds in the team boost performance.

'RELATIONSHIPS ARE like power plays. It's all about control. The moment you let someone get too close, they have power over you. Keep them at arm's length, maintain the upper hand, and you'll never be vulnerable... never let your guard down.'

I love that quote from the character Robert California in the US version of the TV satire *The Office*. It's clearly *not* what relationships are about! But I hope you got a good laugh out of it, too.

The subject of relationships is an important one. Relationships are critical to survival. Even elephants know how important connection is. Ever wondered why they link themselves trunk to trunk? My seven-year-old son explained it to me—so they don't lose each other and their babies won't get eaten by lions. If Robert California were an elephant, he'd cut off his own tail to keep the rest of the herd at arm's length. And then get eaten by a lion. Just as well...

But despite almost every creature on the planet understanding, at least at an instinctive level, how important relationships are, sometimes we forget to nurture them in a work context. They're often forgotten, taken for granted and only addressed when it's too late. And yet research suggests that sixty to seventy per cent of problems in the workplace are caused by interpersonal conflict. One study found that eighty-five per cent of employees experience some form of conflict in the workplace. Interpersonal conflict can occur at all levels of a business, including conflict between managers, supervisors, co-workers or other stakeholders in an organisation.[25]

On the flip side, some organisations put too much emphasis on relationships. Their culture becomes about who you know. Want a quick budget approval? Make sure you know the head of budgeting. Want to bypass compliance testing for a new product? Have a friend in that department. In fact, make sure you know one person in every section—even if there are 176 departments. The problem with this type of culture is that it is not inclusive; it's political and about calling in favours and scratching backs. Some companies like it this way, but it's not fair. People don't follow the process; they work around it. None of this

---

25 https://www.humanxhr.com.au/blog/how-to-manage-interpersonal-conflict

is good for the organisation as a whole but is especially damaging for relationships at the team level.

There's a better way, which is to have a culture of good, healthy relationships. A good, healthy relationship is a great relationship. It's one in which people feel safe. Safe to speak up about anything that's on their mind—problems, issues, risks, concerns, unfair treatment, feeling singled out. A great relationship is a strong relationship. It's one in which people take time out to get to know each other. Healthy relationships make you feel full, not empty. There is safety, trust, commitment and, this may surprise you, conflict. Yes, if you do nothing but agree with each other, it's not a healthy relationship. Conflict is inevitable, and it's not the presence or absence of conflict that determines the strength of a relationship, it's how that conflict is managed. In fact, if there is no conflict, it's possible there's a power play going on and a lack of the psychological safety required to speak up honestly. Relationships are dynamic. Like sharks, if they don't move forward, they die.

Relationships are the lifeblood of teams. Without good relationships, a team is nothing. All the research in this field tells us that relationships are key to wellbeing at work—and everywhere else. Every team-building model under the sun includes a component aimed at improving relationships. Strong relationships are good for productivity. There are multiple payoffs and I could go on forever here. But perhaps the most compelling fact I can share is that people stay in jobs because of the team they're in and leave because of the team they're not in. The most important single factor of high-functioning teams is good relationships. If you want your team to perform well, invest in it. This will help your team to do great. Leading organisations know this.

I often run programs to help organisations improve the relationships within their teams. What's interesting is that the teams in those programs often try to apply some of what I teach to their home life. In fact, ten years ago a multinational health insurance and healthcare company brought me in to support their people to better understand their relationships outside the workplace—that is, friendships and intimate relationships. No doubt about it, relationships are important. They're often the forgotten factor when helping teams through change, they help a team work better together, and the result is better business outcomes.

Making it work

Creating great relationships takes work—ongoing work—and you might need some coaching with this. A good place to start, however, is to look for telltale signs that your relationships are in good shape—or not. You can start by reading through the following 'playbook' and ticking the actions that you deploy to build great relationships in your workplace. (HINT— I'm hoping you don't have too many ticks.)

- [ ] Micromanage your team, breathe down their necks and constantly question their work

- [ ] Ignore your team's efforts

- [ ] Do the bare minimum

- [ ] Publicly criticise others

- [ ] Don't communicate

- [ ] Focus solely on your personal gain

- [ ] Create uncertainty

- [ ] Misuse power

- [ ] Break trust

- [ ] Show disrespect

FIGURE 17 Bad Relationships Playbook

So, how many boxes did you tick?

This 'Bad Relationships Playbook' was inspired by our 'friend' Robert California and the workplace horror stories clients have shared with me. If you ticked any of the boxes, you might want to stop and reflect on the impact these actions are having on your team. If you think you need to work on this, here are my Top Ten Tips to *not* look like Robert California:

1 Give your team space to do their work, and only offer guidance when necessary. Showing you trust them enhances creativity and confidence.

2 Acknowledge the hard work of your team, ensuring they feel valued. Celebrate their efforts and

achievements so that you uplift morale and motivation. Always say thank you.

3   Go the extra mile in your work; this will inspire your team and signal that you're committed.

4   Offer feedback the right way and ensure criticism is constructive. This will protect self-esteem and foster psychological safety within the team.

5   Communicate openly and respectfully. Share information and give your team context or a heads-up of what's coming down the pipeline. This will foster trust within the team.

6   Create a collaborative environment, not a competitive one, where team members feel they're working with each other, rather than against each other.

7   Be candid and open with your team members about where they stand. Be transparent about roles, responsibilities and expectations and make sure everyone is on the same page.

8   Use your power wisely. Good leadership is about empowering people and creating a space where each team member feels valued and encouraged.

9   Trust is fragile. Once broken, it's very hard to regain. Keep your promises and be honest with your team members. Be transparent and reliable and create strong, enduring relationships.

10 Respect others and be kind. This encourages harmony and a positive work atmosphere. Create an environment of mutual respect where contributions are acknowledged and welcomed.

A high-performing team is doing great and doing work that works for everyone. If you feel team performance is slipping, you may need to check that your team relationships are in good shape. Improving relationships by focusing on the ten tips above provides a quick press on the performance pedal that will re-energise your team and keep them on the road to excellence.

CLEAR ROLES

Shift your role, shift the pattern: Gain role clarity to spot the patterns shaping your team and shift dynamics for performance.

IF I asked what your role at work is, I imagine you'd recite what's written on your position description. In our world of work, we no longer have jobs, we have 'roles'. The word 'role', in its true sense, refers to the part or character an actor plays. In a broader sense, it can mean the function we play in society. In no sense is it a list of tasks or accountabilities— but that's often how it's used. Now I'd like to ask again, in the context of the word's true meaning, what is your work 'role'? What 'part' are you playing at work? What is your character's function? Fixer? Do-er? Drama king or queen? (Hope not!) And is playing that role making things better or worse?

Let me tell you about a leader who came to me with a big problem. He had around a hundred people in his team. Big team! He was an operations kinda guy. Practical. Liked results. No fluffing around on his watch. And he was stretched to the max.

'I'm so busy, I've got no time!' he groaned, head in hands. I noticed the stained tie, the crumpled shirt, the unkempt fingernails. The poor guy was obviously so slammed he didn't even have time to do his laundry regularly.

He went on. 'I need more resources. The better managers are reporting to me, but the rest need proper training on how to actually solve problems. It's what they're paid to f****n do, but they're not doing it!'

I asked him to talk me through what was happening.

'They keep coming at me with problems all the time,' he said in frustration. Judging by the fear in his eyes, 'they' could have been ballistic missiles. He went on, 'Absolutely zero thinking behind their problems, no ideas or solutions. Just dumping problems on me. I don't have the time to deal with this s***! That's *their* job!'

'So what do you do when this happens?' I asked.

He shrugged. 'I put their problems on my to-do list and I solve them.'

'Right. How might you be "co-creating" the issue, then?' I asked.

'Huh?'

My answer surprised him, but do you see what's happening here? He was stepping into the role of 'fixer', and because he kept solving his managers' problems this was perpetuating their behaviour. Why would they look for solutions when they knew that dumping problems in their leader's lap would make those problems magically disappear? This is what happens when you assume a 'role'—you cast the other party in a very particular, complementary role, and in doing so influence their behaviour.

Things had to change for this leader. Instead of solving other people's problems, we spoke about how he could shift to asking questions to help the managers think. So he did. The idea was to help his managers come to their own solutions. Which they did. And all the drama stopped. Soon the managers were able to undertake this level of thinking and problem-solving themselves. No more managers crashing into the leader's office and dumping on him. He didn't need more resources. He didn't need better managers. He didn't need to invest in problem-solving and skill-building programs. All he had to do was step out of the role of 'fixer' and into the role of 'leader'. My client had been playing a metaphorical tug-of-war with a monster. Once he dropped his end of the rope—putting his managers' problems on his to-do list—he won the tug-of-war.

There are many roles you might be playing at work—fixer, rescuer, victim, doer, delegator, coach, trainer, counsellor. This is especially true for leaders, who wear many hats. One moment you're directing operations to ensure business outcomes are achieved; the next you're counselling a team member who's going through a rough patch; later you're sharing your knowledge as an expert; the next thing you know you're coaching. One job title, many roles. The list is almost endless, but all roles have one thing in common—the role you step into creates the dynamic of what's happening between the people and the work.

When I left my corporate career and was in the start-up world, I interviewed parents about their relationship challenges. A consistent theme from my problem-discovery interviews was that one person wanted more bedroom action than the other. Over time, this 'desire discrepancy' increased and created issues. What was happening here was that one partner stepped into the role of 'pursuer', which automatically cast the other in the role of 'distancer'. Being the distancer can make someone uncomfortable; they want closeness, not distance. But in this situation the role dynamics force them to create that distance. The relationship will be better served if the pursuer steps out of that role and stops chasing. Stepping out of that role is within the pursuer's control, and it changes the dynamic of what's happening between the couple.

I'll say it again—when you assume a role, you automatically create another role. A hero creates a villain. A fixer creates a problem. Unfortunately, this can create a dynamic that may not be appropriate or constructive. When this happens at work, performance is affected. The team is no longer doing great.

One of the biggest issues I encounter when I interview people in a work context is that their roles and responsibilities aren't clear. When the waters are muddy, there's likely to be duplication of tasks and therefore wasted effort. Conversely, other tasks are neglected. Quality issues are not acknowledged or addressed. If a horse knows which lane it's in, it can just run, but if it's not clear, it'll swerve out of its lane, trip over the other horses and before you know it there are injured horses and concussed jockeys lying all over the track.

Part of my work with leaders and teams involves creating clarity on roles—who's doing what and how is it part of the operating model and way of working? What roles are people stepping into within their jobs? Say a new delivery function is established at a utilities company. There might be initial work to clarify the roles within the new function—who does what, the scope of roles and how the function works—but there could also be a need to look at the roles people had been gifted before the new function was established. Perhaps there was an 'order taker' under a leader who was an 'order giver', but the new function means that dynamic is no longer required. Roles have to be reset to create alignment that suits the new context.

When roles are clear, and everybody knows their part, there are good levels of collaboration, lots of innovation, fast responses to issues and a culture of continuous improvement. All of this adds up to a good hard press on the performance pedal.

You need to find a way to see what role you're playing and what dynamics are at play. Curiosity about the role you're playing or taking on *within* your existing, 'official', role is important here.

It helps to take a fresh perspective. When I was a new mum in my early thirties, I joined a group of other new mums and went along to the 'Reminisce' gig at the Sidney Myer Music Bowl in Melbourne. We were keen to reclaim our youth! We booked tickets for the balcony, where we felt more comfortable as young mums. When the rhythmic, pulsing synth of the upbeat baseline started, the excitement began to build. Connie from Sneaky Sound System came on and launched into a crowd favourite— UFO. And then I saw things in the crowd I'd never seen in my many visits to the Myer Music Bowl. I looked down at the dance floor and saw a group of women starting to engage with a group of men. A guy by himself who women were clearly trying to avoid, and even warning other women about. These dynamics—these roles—were creating some movement and space on the dance floor that I wouldn't have seen if I'd been in the thick of it. My new perspective gave me a fresh view of the roles people were playing.

You can do this in a business context. Step out and up. Create space to see what effect your version of the song 'UFO' is having on the dynamic at play. 'Getting on the balcony' is the term for the mental activity of stepping back from the action and asking, 'What's really going on here?' and 'How could we think about this or work differently together?'[26]

---

26 Heifetz, R., & Linsky, M. (2002). Leadership on the Line: Staying Alive Through the Dangers of Leading. *Harvard Business Review Press*.

It's important to regularly step back from the 'dance of doing' and view how the 'dance is happening'. Viewing ourselves in the dance allows us to shift perspective, change focus, and see what is happening from a wider lens.

If we don't find a way to take a fresh perspective and test our assumptions, we will have a limited view of our reality based only on our own understanding of what's right in front of us. We may fail to understand how others see it or how the whole system is working. This ability to shift perspective is important for individual leaders, but also for leadership teams so they're not 'captive' to their own thinking and ways of working. It allows them to be adaptable and open to change.

Be curious. Step up and out and take in a different view. What can you see happening from this new angle? What's really going on? What are you doing that's perpetuating what's playing out within your team? What role are you taking up?

Making it work

If we want to see a change in behaviour, we need to start by looking at the role and the dynamics it creates. As Joan Lurie once said to me, 'It takes two to create a pattern, but only one to change it.' A role clarity session can be helpful here. This is something that can be tricky to do by yourself, but it is possible. Here's the process.

1 Identify one of your niggles. Describe it fully— get it out of your mind through writing, drawing or taking a voice note. How are things working and not working? Describe it.

2 What part of the niggle seems like the same thing is happening over and over again, almost creating a pattern? This is where taking a new perspective can help uncover the pattern.

3 What assumptions are you holding?

4 What do you make of this?

5 What's a small move you could make that would change this dynamic and disrupt the pattern?

Let's see how this works in practice by taking another look at the example of a new delivery function at a utilities company. Let's say that despite changes in the operating model, a leader keeps going to their preferred person in the shared services area to get the work done. This person has a great relationship with the leader as they've worked together success-fully for the last couple of years. They want to be helpful, so they keep agreeing to the leader's requests for assistance, even though the responsibility now sits with their teammate. By continuing to say 'yes' they're defining their role as 'helper', which is not embedding the new operating model. They need to reframe the role to something like a 'facilitator' or 'connector' so they're not doing the work themselves and taking it away from the person now assigned to that work. By stepping out of one role and into another, they will enable the leader to engage the right person under the new operating model.

You can also run a role clarity session with your team, then follow up with discussions about your responsibility to the team; how your different roles intersect; boundaries that are unclear; and how you see your role. Making roles explicit is the way to create change.

Like many of the practices in the book, this is not 'once and done' like learning to ride a bike—once you get it, you've got it for life—it's an ongoing practice. The more you do it, the better you get. So step up and out and find a position where you can get a fresh perspective. Do this regularly to identify the roles that you and your team are unconsciously stepping into. When everyone is in the right role and staying in that role, work starts to work better for everyone and the team starts doing great.

PART 3

ORGAN- ISATION PRACTICES

WELCOME TO the organisation practices. This is the big-picture stuff. These practices look at what can be done across the whole organisation. It's about shifting how the whole company operates—not just one leader, not just one team or one division, but the whole company. We'll look at structures, processes and strategies, and how the organisation functions and works. This is also where the ideas become more subtle and more challenging. It's where you will be stretched as a leader.

When we look at making work work for organisations, it's complex. Because organisations are complex. They have lots of moving parts. There are so many parts and roles and people and everything that sits between. Chain reactions, cascading waterfalls, ripple effects; they're all possible in our world of work.

The practices in Part 3 roughly equate to the third-tier services in my business. They take longer to implement, they represent the long tail game and results will not be immediate. Patience and commitment are required. Leaders must role-model these traits and be steadfast. These are also the practices that will prepare you for the future of work.

The future is unknown and unknowable until it's upon us, but rest assured it will be even more challenging than the present. You will need to learn to think on your feet, inch forward in the fog and make brave decisions. These practices will all help you build that super-human capacity. You'll need to broaden and deepen your thinking here. You'll need to find a way to think about thinking. This is critical for the future that's just on the horizon. As more tasks in the workplace are automated and AI takes over more of the mundane, leaders will be called upon to do more and more meta-thinking.

As you begin to explore the organisation practices, it's more important than ever to push the right pedal at the right time. Never forget—an organisation can have performance, growth and wellbeing in equal measure. There is no trade-off or sacrifice here. Excellence is in the edges. It sits at the intersection of performance, growth and wellbeing.

I invite you to turn the page and begin to absorb the final practices in this book.

ORGANISATION
WELLBEING

BUILT-IN
WELLBEING

*Build in, don't bolt on: Wellbeing
isn't a workshop. It's part of how
your organisation operates.*

IF YOU walk the corridors of a forward-thinking organisation today, you're likely to find plenty of signs that it cares about the wellbeing of employees. There might be a gym and free showers available to help workers to maintain the stamina they need for their demanding jobs. Perhaps there's a flyer on the noticeboard about an in-house massage therapist, who can coax the knots out of necks bent over laptops for long hours. Sleep pods are tucked into quiet corners so that everyone can get the rest and REM required to stay on top of tight deadlines. The CEO could be joining the midday meditation group, ensuring they have a clear, calm mind to deal with the chaos and craziness of work. 'Wellness' is delivered through one warm and fuzzy initiative after another. But will these initiatives alone create a healthy organisation?

The evidence pile is growing—while wellbeing initiatives at the individual level certainly have some value, they're not sufficient to create organisation-wide wellbeing. A study conducted by William Flemming and published in *Industrial Relations Journal* analysed responses from 46,336 workers across 233 UK organisations, and concluded that those who participated in employee wellbeing programmes were no better off than those who didn't. In fact, they were sometimes worse off.[27] This study joins a growing body of academic literature drawing the same conclusions—that it's wellbeing initiatives implemented at the organisational level that are most likely to produce results.

Wellbeing is not an event. It's an ongoing practice. A fun wedding does not guarantee a strong marriage, and a thirty-minute meditation session in your lunch hour does not support your wellbeing. As Flemming's study concluded, generic, one-size-fits-all wellbeing initiatives are not just a potential waste of resources—they can be harmful. Some common forms of mindfulness, for example, don't work for everyone and can be a difficult practice for some neurodivergent folk. When a practice doesn't work

---

27 Fleming, W. J. (2024) Employee well-being outcomes from individual-level mental health interventions: Cross-sectional evidence from the United Kingdom. *Industrial Relations Journal*. doi.org/10.1111/irj.12418

for an employee, they might think it's somehow their fault. 'Why isn't this working for me? Everyone else loves it... what's wrong with me? Maybe I should keep trying.' It's too easy for employees to blame themselves when their wellbeing is not good. That inner critic gets in their ear and says, 'I'm not resilient enough. I can't handle stress. I'm not pushing back enough. I can't say no.' And then the spiral of blame and shame begins, which isn't good for anyone's wellbeing, let alone the wellbeing of the organisation.

At the time of writing, organisations are spending an estimated $8 million dollars annually on wellbeing initiatives.[28] And there is nothing wrong with providing the means for employees to enhance their wellbeing. There are people who will find sleep pods truly valuable. Others will relish the fully equipped gym. But if workers are using sleep pods because long hours are leaving them so sleep-deprived they can't keep their eyes open in meetings, or because they finished their work by 10:00 am but have to stick around for the afternoon meeting, something is wrong at a systemic level. Work should not reduce wellbeing; it should enhance it.

I believe a paradigm shift is needed. Let's turn this whole approach to wellbeing on its head and see things differently. Creating a sense of wellbeing across an organisation is not an event or a generic

---

28 https://www.linkedin.com/pulse/8-billion-con-why-corporate-wellness-programs-waste-money-van-zyl-oyb4e

practice aimed at individuals. Nor is it achieved by banishing stress from the workplace. Some stress is unnecessary, but some is inevitable, and the right level of stress is actually good for you. What *will* improve organisational wellbeing is a company-wide guarantee that the resources are available to support and enable employees to do their work and the provision of work that is interesting, rewarding and, yes, even challenging.

It's helpful to think about this in terms of withdrawals and deposits, or debits and credits. Work represents the debits on your ledger. The account is drained more quickly when employees grapple with demanding tasks, high workloads, tight deadlines, workplace conflicts, unclear expectations and poorly designed work. Work that creates emotional strain and stress runs up expensive debits. Boring, routine tasks that fail to engage employees can also create a drain on the account. You need to balance all of this by making regular deposits to keep the account in the black. Deposits, or credits, include resources that help employees deal with the demands placed on them and include things like supportive colleagues, adequate training and a positive work environment. Then there are wider factors, such as job security and career development opportunities. Deposits also include interesting and rewarding work that keeps employees engaged. This is about autonomy, choice, control, learning and growth.

Organisational wellbeing is achieved by creating the right conditions, not by adding wellness events.

It is built in—woven into the fabric of an organisation. An employee should feel supported across the entirety of their journey through an organisation, from their onboarding sessions to the day they move on. They should not have to roam the corridors in search of a green smoothie and a neck rub whenever their work is too much or too little. The resources they need to do their job well should be readily available. There should be enough challenge in the work to keep them stimulated. When these factors are present, wellbeing simply emerges across the whole organisation.

Wellbeing initiatives aimed at the organisational level are more likely to achieve results than the warm, fuzzy and expensive interventions aimed at individuals. But creating the conditions for a healthy organisation isn't about ringing a few changes, assuming everyone has what they need to get their job done and then ticking that project off your to-do list. Changes should be intentional, but also sustainable. It's not once and done. It's ongoing and must respond to changing environments, changing work and changing employees.

Changes designed to improve organisational wellbeing must take into account all your employees. I was approached by an organisation with a lot of neurodivergent people in the workforce. The leaders were concerned they weren't up to date with their knowledge and understanding of neurodiversity in the workplace. They asked if I offered any training resources or courses for HR and leaders on 'managing' or 'handling' neurodivergent employees to ensure they were coping well. A one-hour 'lunch and learn' session was suggested. The answer was yes, of course I can help you here, but you need more.

The needs of this group of leaders, and any neurodivergent person, are not all the same and can't be gathered under a single umbrella. I explained that they needed to change mindsets and create an environment and space where everyone has their needs met so they can bring out their best. Efforts to accommodate the needs of neurodivergent folk must be infused and designed as part of the full HR life cycle. This starts with how you recruit, how you deliver your learning programs, how you develop and grow your leaders, and so on. You need more than something separate that just hangs off to the side, like a lunch and learn. If you're going to be serious and committed to building wellbeing, you need to design it into the work. It's not a once-and-done event. But it's certainly a start.

Making it work

Building wellbeing into an organisation requires three steps that repeat in ongoing cycles.

1 **Check account balance**: Regularly assess the withdrawals placed on employees to determine where they're coming from and how 'expensive' they are. Do this by conducting surveys, holding feedback sessions and monitoring workloads to identify stressors.

2 **Deposit resources**: Top up resources and tweak support systems to help employees manage demands. These include training programs, ensuring access to necessary tools and facilitating a supportive work culture. It also includes providing enough stimulating work.

3 **Monitor levels**: Continuously check that enough deposits are being made to maintain viability. Implement regular check-ins, promote open communication and adjust resources as needed.

DEPOSITS (+)	WITHDRAWALS (-)
Supportive resources & environment	Stressors & demands
• Supportive colleagues • Adequate training • Positive work environment • Career development opportunities • Interesting and rewarding work • Autonomy • Learning and growth opportunities • Resources that help employees deal with job demands	• Demanding tasks • High workloads • Tight deadlines • Workplace conflicts • Unclear expectations • Poorly designed work • Tasks that create emotional strain and stress • Boring, routine tasks that fail to engage employees

FIGURE 18 Ledger of Wellbeing

Potential stressors must be addressed before they become overwhelming. Tools and support available to employees must be continuously enhanced. But most critically, sustainable practices must be implemented to ensure that wellbeing is built into the organisation. In such a haven, employees will thrive—as will the organisation. When wellbeing ambitions are embraced at a company level and recognised as a fundamental responsibility of leaders, it is a step towards excellence. That excellence will send its ripples out into the wider community and beyond. Be aware of the power you wield here. You truly can make an impact. You can make work work for everybody.

HUMAN-CENTRIC CHANGE

Lead change, prioritise wellbeing: Leadership during change must prioritise wellbeing for compliance and performance.

THIS IS the section of the book where the rude words will be found. In particular, one word so awful that I've been asked not to use it. Yes, the c-word: CHANGE.

Looming change initiatives can strike terror into the hearts of hapless employees. At the project or portfolio level, poorly managed change can feel like being caught in a hailstorm without an umbrella. Directives and emails and instructions and surveys and new procedures start raining down from above. There is a lot to read and initiate and absorb. The ground becomes saturated and people start slipping and sliding in the mud. There can be conflict and contradiction. Often there is no consultation, no communication, no clear goals and no detail about what's changing. Information is confused and disorganised. In an environment like this, rumours abound. Are those storm clouds bringing redundancies?

As the storm of change whips up, the hailstones get bigger and the rain starts coming in sideways. Every work stream has a new initiative. Everyone is doing all this f***ing... 'stuff'. But what is actually adding value? It's separate, separate, separate. Where is the integration? When everybody is stuck in siloes, you might find five different teams working on the exact same initiative.

And then there's the imperative for the change to look good and make the change-maker look good. Precious resources are thrown into branding the change and baking frigging cupcakes to celebrate it. But this just reinforces the siloes. Overwhelmed people start jumping ship. Those who stay put and keep rowing begin to feel overwhelmed. Leaders, too. Everybody is distracted. This frenzy inevitably affects productivity and morale and threatens the wellbeing of the organisation as a whole.

But it doesn't have to be this way.

Change can be transformative and exciting. It's the path forward. And done right, it's awesome.

Good change spawns many wonders—new products, new revenue lines, more free time and more meaningful work. A change such as new tech that creates greater efficiency frees up more time for life-enhancing activities—just make sure those new laptops are loaded with the right programs and free of bugs before you roll them out! A change that removes admin tasks from a sales role gives the salespeople more time to spend with... well... people. Changes to ways of working can be beneficial. Just look at how many people have embraced hybrid working in recent years. Moving away from a rigid nine-to-five workday helps employees with a 'night owl' chronotype follow their natural sleep cycle and perform at their best.

The benefits of properly led change are undeniable. I helped coordinate a major change for a multinational company that involved twenty tech projects and affected 35,000 people. Integrating that change saved twenty-eight days' worth of work for the company. Had it not been properly managed and integrated, employees would have spent twenty-eight days away from customers and not doing their jobs. With the change done well, productivity was maintained and the change itself laid the path for future growth.

And what about wellbeing? Isn't that what we're talking about here? Indeed it is. The detriment to wellbeing of poorly led change is clear. Slipping and sliding in the mud is a good way to break bones and crack open skulls. In fact, poor change management is one of the most commonly experienced psychosocial hazards in Australia. This is such an important issue that managing change well is now a legal requirement. The code of practice that became effective in 2023 provides specific guidance for companies to mitigate the hazard of poor organisational change management. In other words, it's official: inadequate communication and support during organisational changes can lead to uncertainty and stress. And this is a hazard.

But it doesn't have to be. The opposite is also true—well-managed change *enhances* wellbeing. And did you know that wellbeing also affects the success of a change initiative? When the wellbeing of an organisation is good, there are higher levels of energy and this can be channelled into the change. When that change is done well, it further enhances organisational wellbeing, which makes the next change easier to implement, and on and on in a virtuous cycle. Change and wellbeing are intertwined. They go together like peaches and cream—or macaroni and cheese, if you have a savoury tooth. But whatever the flavour, wellbeing and change are symbiotic, and this is a key fact I want you to remember.

Change is a high-stakes game and its success depends in large part on a leader's ability to implement it. As a leader, you have people's health in your hands. How you go about creating change is critical. This affects both wellbeing and the success of the change. There must be trust and safety. If you need help in this high-stakes game, don't be afraid to ask for it. I'm often approached by leaders to guide them through change management. It's my bread and butter, and I can help you.

Making it work

Remember, you need to comply with the Code of Practice. This means that:

- Communication must be effective. That is, it must be timely and clear and include reasons for the change, the expected outcomes and the timeline.

- Employees must be involved. You must seek their input and feedback to minimise uncertainty and resistance.

- Support systems must be in place. This includes such things as access to counselling services, training for new roles or systems and opportunities for employees to discuss concerns.

- The impact of the change on employees must be monitored and reviewed. If required, adjustments must be made to reduce stress and maintain wellbeing.

Compliance is critical, but now I want to take things further and look at what you, personally, can do at a behavioural level to ensure a smooth and successful change that keeps wellbeing front and centre.

First, here are a few don'ts and one very important do:

- Don't dismiss people's feelings—all feelings are valid, whether they're rational or irrational. Silly feelings don't go away when you tell their owner they're silly.

- Don't think you can change people's behaviour single-handedly. Thoughts, feelings, the internal environment (e.g. nervous system) and the external environment (e.g. workplace) all play a role in people's behaviour.

- Don't tell people to focus on the positives and be grateful they still have their jobs, or that they're paid well, yadda, yadda, yadda…

- Don't tell people to either get on board or get lost. Ultimatums don't help anyone.

- Don't prevaricate, vacillate or obfuscate… Get it? Clear is kind.

- Don't avoid certain words because you don't want people to make a certain association. This damages trust. 'It's not change, it's transformation,' won't fool anyone. Safety is built on trust and trust is built on honesty.

- Do validate people's feelings. Everybody will react differently to the change—some positive, some negative and many in between. Whatever someone's experience, it's okay.

During periods of change, people will look to their leaders for reassurance. When change is difficult, there are tools you can use to support the wellbeing of both yourself and your team. The trick is to learn those tools in your downtime—*before* the change is upon you. Get ahead by learning these tools in the off season so that you can readily deploy them when you're in the thick of the match and in danger of slipping in the muddy ground.

As a leader, you may have developed some tools to support your wellbeing through change. What are they? Can you model and share these with those around you? They might find them useful. Or they might have their own techniques. No need to force stuff down people's throats here—they've got enough stuff on their plates.

Having worked in the field of change myself for almost two decades, I have many tools to help me deal with overwhelm and uncertainty. Here are some common ones that resonate that you might like to try and then share:

- Focus your time and energy on what you *can* control and influence, not what you can't.

- Try moving when you're stressed. Stretching helps, as well as busting some really bad dance moves to really loud, really daggy music.

- Step back from thoughts when those thoughts are full of fear and uncertainty. It's like being at a sushi train restaurant. You don't have to eat every morsel that goes by; the idea is to choose the ones you want. Likewise, choose which thoughts to get on board with.

- Try creating some word vomit. I get out a big sheet of blank paper and go gangbusters drawing and writing down everything that's on my mind. The goal is just to get it all out—like when you're nauseated and you know vomiting will make you feel better. This helps create separation. I look at the 'vomit' and see that it's not part of me. Then I can do something with it... usually dissect it, categorise it and create a bit of a plan.

- Knowing when your thoughts are caught in a mind trap and knowing how to get them out of that trap is also important. Mind traps include things like jumping to conclusions, mind reading and catastrophising. Have you seen the movie *Entrapment* with Catherine Zeta-Jones? There's a scene where she breaks into a Scottish castle to steal a priceless Chinese mask. To get to the mask she must expertly weave her way through red security laser beams with the agility and flexibility of a cat. I conjure that scene and imagine myself ducking and weaving like Catherine to avoid getting caught in the mind traps threatening to ensnare me. The leather suit is optional.

Manage change badly and the results can be catastrophic. Do change well, and you experience enhanced wellbeing. Either way, change is a powerful force, and with great power comes great responsibility. Make sure you use your power for good. Help make work work for everyone and move your organisation towards excellence.

POWERFUL ENGAGEMENT

Triple focus, triple engagement:
Use performance, growth and
wellbeing conversations to
build employee engagement.

ROLL UP! Roll up! Time for the annual employee engagement survey! Get your tickets here for a chance to have your say!

Engagement surveys are a staple of the corporate world. They have many names...

'Your Say'... 'My Say'... 'Speak Up'... 'Step Up'... 'Your Voice'... 'Our Voice... 'Our Culture'... 'Your Culture'

... but they have one purpose: to deepen employee engagement and thus drive culture and performance. But what about wellbeing?

Employee engagement surveys provide important data for organisations, and data can tell an organisation how well things are working. They're a pulse check on strategy. They allow measurements to be taken, which can indicate whether an initiative is working over time, or how different teams are performing. An engagement survey can indicate where something needs nudging or tweaking. Surveys can also pull out the big themes. Occasionally an organisation can be blindsided by the results. Great, they know to revisit a strategy and perhaps make a pivot.

But there's also a downside to engagement surveys. Done annually, surveys only provide a snapshot of a moment in time. A lot can change in a year, and this makes the utility of a survey questionable. There can be pressure to achieve high participation rates— sometimes 100% is the target. But if done too frequently, participation will drop. There can be pressure on employees to give a good impression. Sadly, employees sometimes avoid giving honest answers. If they dare to tell the unvarnished truth, the task of addressing the problems they raise might be thrown right back at them. Ouch.

Surveys cost a lot of money and time. They have to be rolled out and completed. The results have to be unpacked, debriefs have to happen, follow-up communication is required. There is a cascade of work here. Are we getting good ROI? Is there bang for the buck?

Most critically, results have to be interpreted. And I mean interpreted correctly. Data doesn't always reveal the right answer to the problem it identifies. For example, let's say an engagement survey uncovers employees' desire to improve work/life balance.

Great! Problem identified and solution obvious—deploy training in work/life balance. Really? What if we dig a little deeper? Perhaps what the employees really want is a workplace where they can be more focused and productive. What will help to achieve that? Again, let's take a good look around. It could be that something as simple as reporting work status is taking up egregious amounts of time. Will work/life balance training fix that? No, but an intervention such as a user-friendly, integrated online reporting system may well be able to and therefore will have greater impact than generic training.

The problems start when engagement becomes the strategy. Engagement is not a strategy. It is a data point that informs strategy. And data is neither good nor bad. It's just information. The goal is not to improve the measurements in next year's or next month's survey. The goal is to use the data points you have to help you better understand your organisation and its challenges. Let's say ten out of 1,500 people in an organisation complain that they can't find the resources they need on the intranet. Okay, yes, that's frustrating for them. And if you fix that issue, you'll have a clean, clear and measurable improvement in next year's survey. But really—will this lift the bar for the whole organisation? And sometimes bonuses are connected to engagement results. That $30,000 bonus for improving results makes it tempting to focus on, well, improving results.

Engagement is not strategy. Engagement is not culture. The fact is that the most important factor in an employee's engagement is their relationship with their direct leader. Engagement surveys are here to stay, and so they should be—their data is important—but you should hold that data lightly. In striving for true engagement, you need to embed quality interactions between employees and their direct managers. This is good news because it means that creating engagement is easier than you think.

Making it work

So what does it take to actively engage? Conversation. (I'll pause here so you can take a moment to face-palm). To engage, we need to talk. And we need to be constantly having three specific types of conversations with the people in our teams. This goes well beyond simply scheduling regular performance reviews. You need to have ongoing, consistent and powerful conversations that allow employees to reflect on how they're doing while integrating the three pedals of excellence—performance, growth and wellbeing. Ask your people:

- How are you feeling?
- How are you doing?
- How are you getting better?

	Question	Measurement Tool
Wellbeing	**How are you feeling?**	Energy/Battery charge
Performance	**How are you doing?**	Outcomes/Benefits
Growth	**How are you getting better?**	Skills/Capacity

FIGURE 19 Engaging 1:1 Conversations

In practice, this should be done in a structured way. An employee should take some time to reflect on these questions and write out their answers, then share them with their leader before meeting for their one-on-one conversation. This is important. Although these three questions are simple, they're designed to go deep. It's not about ambushing an employee without notice, firing a few questions at them and getting some quick, on-the-spot answers. If you do that, you'll get answers like 'Yeah, good, pretty well, I dunno.' Not exactly deep! The aim is to boost self-awareness, which aids critical thinking and can be protective. It's a way to process experiences and manage stress, which prevents burnout.

By using this approach you're essentially doubling down on engagement. The questions provide a scaffolding that helps an employee to reflect and engage with their experience of work. And then, when the leader has the conversation and they discuss the reflections, it creates further engagement.

As a leader, these conversations can frame and

inform your regular one-on-ones. Asking your team members how they're doing relates to performance. The answer to this can be found in the work and tends to be built in via regular performance reviews and so on. There is an operating rhythm to this. Conversations about growth sometimes happen on the back of performance conversations, as they can be linked. At other times the employee is responsible for driving growth, and so there's a separation. Feedback convos fit into this category.

It's not always easy for people to reflect on and ponder these matters. When it comes to wellbeing, you might find you need a language, a way to describe wellbeing while acknowledging that health and wellbeing mean different things to different people. The concept of a battery is helpful here. Batteries provide energy. Energy is at the heart of wellbeing. This idea of personal energy is not new—we all know that some things give us energy and other things/people/tasks/thoughts take it away. As the mother of a child with a nervous system disability, I am acutely aware of this. I have learnt through hands-on experience that to ensure she is engaged at school—that is, participating—her battery must not be depleted.

Using the concept of energy as a proxy for wellbeing is helpful. We can talk about our battery charge and where it's at. What's draining it and what's energising it? What's the current charge at? Ask this question when you have the wellbeing conversation. It's important to keep monitoring this so that you can act before it's too late. Like the time I was mid presentation and the light on my keyboard started flashing. It was a warning signal. I didn't know what it was at the time; I was in flow, focused on the audience, delivering my messages, answering their questions. But that red flash was a warning sign that the battery on my cordless keyboard was running out of juice and about to cark it. Having a regular conversation with your co-workers about wellbeing is the equivalent of monitoring the battery on your cordless keyboard. It provides the active awareness that allows you to act before it's too late.

Together, these three conversations—about performance, growth and wellbeing—have their own signal. That you care, that this is important, that this is what you're all about. Through this, engagement is created. And when you have engagement, the wellbeing of the whole organisation is enhanced, your people feel good, work starts to work for everyone, and we all reap the rewards of excellence.

ORGANISATION GROWTH

LOOK BEFORE
YOU LEAP

Every action has a reaction: leaders must look at the whole system to avoid unintended consequences.

REMOVING A BLOCK from a Jenga tower can be simple enough, but if you don't consider the structure as a whole, the entire tower might come crashing down.

It's the same with an organisation. We're trained in leadership development, but we don't always develop the sense to look at the organisation holistically—to see into the cracks, see the glue critical for growth. We often see the parts, the roles, the people, but we miss the in-between—the connections that are vital. And this is dangerous.

If we want to make work work, we need a new lens on leadership. Let's look outside our organisations for a moment and consider what family life, Netflix and the Ring of Fire can teach us about systems leadership and the 'in-between'.

In my family of four, each of us takes on different roles: mum, wife, dad, husband, son, brother, daughter and sister. Say my husband, Josh, and I have a disagreement or argument. How we communicate and manage our conflict shapes the emotional environment at home. It could be toxic, tense or tranquil. This 'emotional environment' is the in-between space, and it's crucial because it affects our children's sense of safety.

Netflix's *Stranger Things* features 'The Upside Down', a twisted parallel dimension of our real world that's dark and full of creatures and events that can't be explained. In the show, a group of kids face various obstacles as they try to navigate between the real world and the Upside Down and deal with the connections between these realms.

Or take Sal and Franco, who have been happily married for a while but are now facing difficulties. They decide to go to marriage counselling. Who does the therapist say is the client? Sal? Franco? No. The client is the marriage—the in-between.

The Pacific Ring of Fire is an area in the Pacific Ocean where the movement of tectonic plates creates intense seismic activity. There are frequent earthquakes and volcanic eruptions, which are destructive but also create fertile land and new islands. This dynamic activity all takes place where the plates meet—it's in the in-between. Similarly, the dynamic shifts within an organisation, driven by hidden connections, can lead to both challenges and opportunities for growth.

So the 'in-between' is literally in between. It's the emotional environment, the connection between realms, the marriage, the fault lines at the edges of tectonic plates. It's what sits in between and connects the parts, the roles, the people. It's in this in-between space where challenges often lie. The challenge isn't with Sal or Franco individually; it's with the marriage. Challenges rarely exist in the parts alone.

It's the same for an organisation. Leaders must recognise that this in-between space provides a mechanism for growth—it's a key driver for effectiveness. But too often, leadership training falls short and leaders are wired for simplicity. We often overlook these interconnections, rendering us unable to leverage this 'glue' for sustainable growth. Without seeing these connections, leaders make decisions that lead to unintended consequences. We get trapped in focusing on our own patch, seduced into siloed thinking and operating—doing our own thing, managing up and down, without considering how it interacts across the whole organisation.

Why does this happen? Seeing interconnections and managing them is complex. They're harder to see and not as easy to measure and monitor as other KPIs or scorecards.

But as Joan Lurie says, 'Leaders must be system leaders, not just people leaders.'

Grow your leaders to grow your organisation. Leaders must develop to effectively manage the interconnections within the organisation. This is essential for sustainable growth. Every action has a reaction—making a change in one area affects another part of the organisation. You need to be aware of this so that you can be on the lookout for unintended consequences.

I learnt this lesson the hard way. I was trying to shed a few kilos but still had a major sweet tooth. So I stocked up on sugar-free lollies from the chemist, thinking I could go nuts on them since they were low in sugar. Turns out you can't. I was so focused on cutting out sugar that I didn't consider what I was replacing it with and how it'd affect my body in high doses. Those artificial sweeteners seemed like a harmless swap, but they wreaked havoc. Nothing like stomach cramps and diarrhoea to teach you the lesson of unintended consequences.

Every action has a reaction, and if you don't consider the whole system, you might just end up in a world of pain.

So, how does this play out in the workplace?

Imagine the exec who asks, 'Who's doing innovation?' Turns out nobody is, so they create a new 'Growth and Innovation' function and hire a star to be the Head of Innovation. Right, that's who does innovation. It's sorted.

Soon enough, the innovation team is overwhelmed with requests, and there's dysfunction within their team. The growth that was supposed to be spawned from this isn't happening. Performance isn't looking too good, either.

The exec comes into the quarterly business performance review. 'Right, we're stagnating in some parts of the organisation. We're not innovating, not getting better according to any of our metrics. What's going on here?'

They all point to Innovation and say, 'We're not responsible for innovation and growth—they are.'

The Head of Innovation stands up, takes a whiteboard marker in hand, and sketches how she sees innovation happening in the organisation. It's not an org chart. It's a picture of how it hangs together in her mind. Pointing to her drawing, she explains, 'Product is where my team innovates. Not in tech, operations, not our learning programs, not in our equipment. But innovation is dispersed throughout all our roles. We all have a role to play.'

It clicks with HR first. 'It's like in HR—I'm not responsible for leadership behaviour across the whole organisation.'

And Finance adds, 'I'm not the only person responsible for all the money.'

Can you see what happened here? The exec created a new innovation function so the organisation could be more innovative in the product space and become a market driver by anticipating what customers need before they know themselves. The unintended consequence was that leaders in other functions neglected innovation in their respective areas because they thought it sat with the new function. The upshot was little growth and unmet performance targets.

Instead, the exec should have looked at the whole system when they created the new innovation function. They should have looked at the interconnections and the in-between bits. Rather than asking, 'Who is going to do innovation?', the challenge should have been, 'How do we make innovation work across all roles and speed up innovation throughout the organisation?'

Another example comes from the rise of remote working. A company might shift to 100% remote work to increase flexibility and employee satisfaction. An unintended consequence could be decreased team collaboration and communication that leads to siloes and a drop in innovation.

To avoid unintended consequences, effectively manage tensions and trade-offs, and achieve planned payoffs—the foundation for growth—you must anticipate the ripple effects. Not just the immediate effects but long-term reactions too. But to anticipate the earthquakes and eruptions, you've got to see the fault lines first.

As the saying goes, 'Mind the cracks—or you might expose one of your own!'

You need to look before you leap. And to look, you need to see the system.

Making it work

Here's a five-step process I've designed to ensure you're looking before you leap. Each step involves understanding a key principle and then going through a checklist to ensure you have it under consideration.

1 See the big picture

Principle: Start by understanding the broader context. Don't just focus on your own area; look at how everything fits together within the whole system.

Checklist:

- Are you considering the entire system, not just your own part?

- Have you framed the challenge with the bigger picture in mind?

2 Know your role

Principle: Get clear on what your role is and how it connects with others in the organisation. Understand how your actions affect the bigger picture.

Checklist:

- What's your part in all this?

- How do your actions link up with what others are doing?

3 **Spot the in-between**

Principle: Focus on the relationships and interactions that hold everything together. Pay attention to the connections that aren't always obvious.

Checklist:

- What are the key connections that could be affected?

- How are different parts of the system linked in this scenario?

4 **Think beyond just now**

Principle: Consider who's affected by your decisions and think about the long-term impact. Don't just act in the moment—think ahead.

Checklist:

- Who's going to feel the impact of this decision?

- Who might you need to engage?

- What are the potential payoffs or consequences down the line?

5 **Check your thinking**

Principle: Keep questioning your assumptions and exploring other options. Make sure your decisions are well-rounded and informed.

Checklist:

- What assumptions are you making?
- What other options have you thought about?
- How might others see this situation?
- What could happen if you go with this plan?

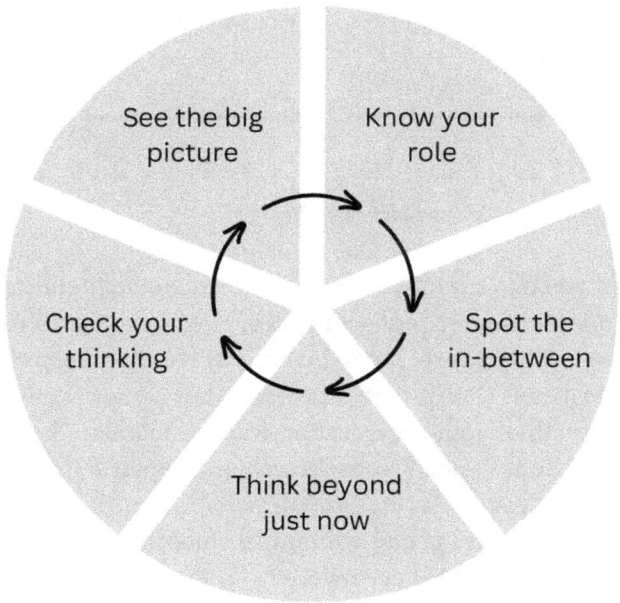

FIGURE 20 How to Look Before You Leap

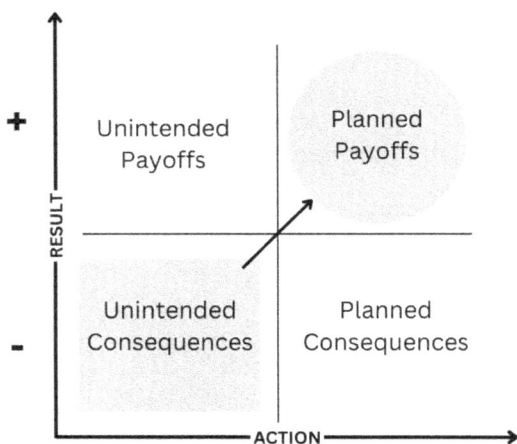

FIGURE 21 Consequences vs Payoffs

If you don't want your actions to create unintended and unwanted consequences, you need to look before your leap. It can be hard to see the interconnections—the in-between spaces, but if you can, the growth of your organisation will be steadier. There will be less need to backtrack and repair damage. When you press the growth pedal using this practice, the road ahead will unfurl smoothly and lead you straight to excellence.

BE CONSTANTLY CURIOUS

*Curiosity drives growth: Unlearn
what you think you know to ask
the questions that create change.*

IMAGINE YOU OPEN a chocolate bar, and inside, nestled between the foil and the paper wrapper, is a golden ticket. That ticket opens the door to a famous, yet mysterious chocolate factory. Inside the gates you find a world of pure imagination, where extraordinary treasures abound and nothing is as it seems. Lickable wallpaper, rivers flowing with chocolate, edible toadstools. Gosh, how I'd love to explore Willy Wonka's world of pure imagination. But please bear with me...

Suppose you look at that bright red toadstool with pure white spots and recognise it as a deadly species. And it is a deadly species—in the world outside the chocolate factory's gates. But within the factory's walls, that toxic-looking toadstool is a sweet, delectable and harmless treat. To see that, to know that you must be open to new ideas—you must be curious.

Curiosity may have killed the cat—perhaps when it ate that delectable-looking toadstool—but it won't kill your organisation. In fact, curiosity is an important factor in organisational growth.

What is curiosity? In essence, it's unlearning. I'm sorry if that statement makes you feel like squirming. You've spent years learning how to lead. School, university, graduate studies, further studies. Learning on the job. Always learning on the job. And all that learning is vital. But sometimes it gets in your way because learning is a curiosity killer. You need to know when to put all that learning aside and rediscover childlike curiosity.

Yes, there's an element of uncertainty here, but that's good! There's even an element of humility and vulnerability to this. I recall one very smart, very competent leader I was talking to about curiosity. When I brought this up, she laughed and said, 'Cognitively—you know, in my brain—I know I don't have to have all the answers. Nobody does. But if I'm being really honest, I *feel* like I do!' I get it. You're in your role for a reason. People have expectations of you. You don't want to appear ignorant. You're supposed to know stuff. But it's okay not to. When you don't know stuff, you can be curious. You can unleash your fascination with everything.

Curiosity is a defining trait of exceptional and gifted people. They tend to ask deeper and more probing questions. They have a strong desire to understand complex concepts and solve problems. Ada Lovelace, considered to be the first computer programmer and the only legitimate child of the poet Lord Byron, was such a person. She had a deep curiosity about the mechanical calculating machine English mathematician Charles Babbage invented. This curiosity led her to write the first algorithm intended for a machine as she envisioned how it could be used for complex tasks such as composing music. Here we see how curiosity laid the groundwork for the future of computer science. If you want to grow your organisation, I suggest you get curious.

Curiosity manifests in questions. Need a solution to a problem? Start by asking questions—genuinely curious questions. Not questions you know the answers to—that's what lawyers do in court. Lawyers want a conviction, and questions like this can be a death sentence for organisational growth.

You need to ask questions before settling on the answers. Again, this might sound idiotically obvious. Of course you ask a question before answering it. But is this really what's happening in your organisation? To answer that question, ask this one:

Are answers coming
before questions?

You need to define a problem before you solve it. You need to use divergent thinking before you converge on an answer. Do not pass 'GO' before you're thoroughly prepared for your journey.

Let's go back to Willy Wonka's world of pure imagination for a moment. Think of curiosity as an Everlasting Gobstopper—the revolutionary treat that Willy Wonka created that lasted forever. And the more you sucked, the more flavours and colours emerged. It's a good metaphor for a curious mind, which continually seeks out new experiences and new knowledge. It's multi-dimensional. It's full of surprises. It's always interesting and leaves you in awe. This is the mindset I want you to immerse yourself in before you settle on answers. Think of your problems and issues and projects as an Everlasting Gobstopper. Because the way you understand your problems will influence your answers and solutions.

While asking questions carries minimal risk— in theory—people in the corporate world who ask 'What is the problem we're solving for?' or 'Why are we doing this?' can become outcasts. When you question the status quo, or why something is being done, it's a big thing. It makes the elephant in the room visible. It questions the wisdom of having spent all that money. You can lose your job and incite politics and scandal. But that's another reason to ask questions *before* implementing solutions.

The start-up world is where I have often seen solutions chasing a problem. One example was a teddy bear that replicated a pregnant mother's heartbeat. You could feel the little teddy pulsating when you cuddled it. We all thought it was really cool. Except one of the more experienced entrepreneurs in the accelerator program asked what problem this cute little teddy was solving. He thought it was a great idea, but unless it solved a problem there wouldn't be a market for it. The entrepreneurs in residence decided to go back to the consumers. It wasn't a case of going back to the 'drawing board' and looking for another product, but going back to parents and doing problem-discovery interviews to find a product/market fit.

Making it work

Let's get out of our imagination for a moment and look at how this works in reality. Say a mortgage broker has a growth goal. They want to increase profits. They might be thinking: 'If I can hire a few more client services managers, they can eventually become brokers, which will help the business grow and increase profitability. At the moment, if I go down, it all goes down with me. How do I minimise key person risk? How do I find good people to train into brokers? The market's competitive, and it's had to find good people.'

What's the problem here, as defined by this business owner? In a nutshell, it's 'How can I find good people to hire?' The answers to this question might include: word of mouth, referrals, I'll keep an eye out. But is that business owner asking the right question?

A better question... a curious question inspired by the Everlasting Gobstopper... could be: 'How might we grow the business and increase profitability with less reliance on me?' This question produces different answers. Employing more people as brokers becomes just one possible solution. Others include cost cutting, and diversifying into accounting, financial planning, products, public speaking, and so on.

Curiosity is a strength, and like a muscle, it can be built up with practice. Start thinking in questions. Have the words 'How might we...' on the tip of your tongue at all times. Make sure a question precedes every action. Try to resist the urge to close the gap on uncertainty. Sometimes you have to put on the brakes and slow down to speed up. Try to learn something new every day. Be on the lookout for alternatives.

Again, asking questions is at the heart of curiosity. The right question is like the combination that unlocks the safe where the best solutions are lurking.

Here's a five-step process I've developed, which I call the 'Curiosity Check: Align Answers and Questions':

1. Start by looking at your current top three priorities, projects or activities.
2. Ask yourself what question each of these is attempting to answer.
3. Now ask each team member what they think each of these questions is attempting to answer. Ask your team members separately – you want honest, unfiltered opinions here.
4. Now compare the answers. Do they align? If not, you may be asking the wrong questions. Get curious and ask fresh ones.
5. Rinse and repeat.

FIGURE 22 Curiosity Check: Align Answers & Questions

Curiosity helps move you forward. It's the path to growth and staying relevant. It's the road to innovation. It will help move an organisation towards balanced excellence. This is transformational. Questions are the behavioural expression of curiosity. Growth is impossible without curiosity. Make sure your questions are the right ones before you settle on the answers. Curiosity may have killed the cat— but do you know the second part of that adage? No? There is an often-overlooked second part to the saying: 'Curiosity killed the cat, but satisfaction brought it back.' You may perceive that curiosity is dangerous, but the fulfilment of finding answers can be worth the risk. It may be that quick press on the growth pedal that your organisation needs to start getting better.

GUIDE YOUR
GROWTH[29]

*Use coaching conversations to expand
perspectives, guide growth and lead change.*

YOU MAY remember a viral meme from a few years
ago—2015 to be precise—that involved a striped
bodycon dress and almost broke the internet. What
was not so precise about this dress was the colour.
Black and blue? Or white and gold? I know you
have a perspective on this. I mean, *everybody* did.

It all started when a Scottish woman named
Cecelia Bleasdale sent her daughter Grace a picture
of a dress she'd seen in a shop that she planned to
wear to Grace's upcoming wedding. The dress, said
the mother of the bride, was black and blue. When
Grace opened the photograph, however, she saw
a dress that was white and gold. The picture was

---

29 Dr Michael Cavanagh and Dr Travis Kemp need to be thanked and acknowledged here. They have shaped my thinking and whole way of being in life.

duly posted on Facebook so that Grace's friends could confirm the colour of the dress, but they were divided about what they saw—some saw black and blue and some saw white and gold. And the viral sensation was born.

Soon the whole world was talking about it. Celebrities weighed in: Justin Bieber thought it was blue and black, as did Taylor Swift, whose tweet in which she said she was 'scared and confused' by the reality-challenging dress was retweeted over 100,000 times. In one twenty-four-hour period, the dress was the subject of 4.4 million tweets. At least three scientific studies attempting to explain and learn from this phenomenon have been conducted and published in respected journals. That's right—actual scientific journals.

In fact, the dress was black and blue, but that's not the point. The point is that we all see things differently; we have different perspectives. I've coached leaders and teams across hundreds of organisations, and every time I start working with a new client I encounter a new perspective. I also often learn something from new clients. When that black and blue dress broke the internet, people learnt a lot about colour perception differences and how lighting and context can affect what they see. This story is a perfect illustration of what happens when two viewpoints about a single subject collide, and the ensuing discussion gives birth to fresh perspectives and brand-new ideas.

When you're pressing on that growth pedal, seeking and discovering new perspectives is important.

But don't worry, I'm not going to make you stare at a white and gold dress while I try to convince you it's black and blue. What I am going to do is explain why coaching—or guided growth, as I like to call it—is the perfect vehicle for finding those fresh perspectives and one you can turn to when you want to focus on growing and getting better.

There are many types of coaching. Remedial coaching is for fixing issues. For example, if Jenny from the Block was failing to hit those high notes, she'd hire a voice coach. Performance coaching focuses on helping the recipient achieve targets. If J.Lo needed to gain x kilos of muscle to prepare for an upcoming tour, she'd hire a personal trainer, nutritionist and chef. And then there's developmental coaching. Developmental coaching looks at how we structure our world—what our assumptions and perspectives are, in both the broad and strategic sense. Personally, how do we sit in the world? In J.Lo's case, this might involve hiring a coach to help her grow and develop as a person. And that personal development might help her sort out her issues with Ben Affleck and save her from the heartache of a fourth divorce! But jokes aside, it's *developmental* coaching that I'm talking about here.

There's also the question of where the coaching takes place. As a coach, you might think that my job is to parachute into an organisation, apply my secret weapons to the problem at hand in a take-no-prisoners kind of way, then gather my kit and slip into the night to rendezvous with the helicopter waiting to drop me into my next mission. And that is part of what I do. Bringing in external coaches can be the right move for an organisation. Coaching can also be done internally, meaning that an employee does the coaching within an organisation. I've also been an internal coach and guided many leaders and organisations through change.

Often leaders are encouraged to skill up in coaching, and I'm sometimes brought in to teach leaders how to coach. You may have had coaching on coaching yourself. Perhaps you've learnt a model or two, which you can use for short, on-the-spot coaching sessions, for longer conversations, or as follow-up to feedback. This is great. We want a coaching approach to leadership.

But wait, there's more—and I don't mean steak knives. I believe there is untapped value here in the form of peer-to-peer coaching.

Peer-to-peer coaching has a special quality, or rather it's free of a particular quality. No matter how skilled a leader is, when they coach individuals at a lower rank in their organisation, there can be a power imbalance. When your line manager is your coach, for example, you can feel like you're being evaluated. This is not the safest context in which to grow professionally and can limit learning.[30] Even if that power imbalance is not real and just perceived,

---

30 Ladyshewsky, R., & Taplin, R. (2017). Employee perceptions of managerial coaching and work engagement using the Measurement Model of Coaching Skills and the Utrecht Work Engagement Scale. *International Journal of Evidence Based Coaching and Mentoring,* 15(2), 25–42.

this fact limits the effectiveness of the coaching. Connection is important for coaching. Rapport needs to be present. With peers, this can be achieved more easily.

Coaching takes place through conversations. The secret weapon embedded in a good coaching conversation is the balance of challenge and support that ultimately leads to new ways of thinking and new insights. That balance is easier to achieve among peers.

Let's look at an example to see how this can play out in practice and the value that can be left behind when perspectives are not sought. Say you've got a problem with work-life balance. You work too many hours and have no time for yourself, but you love your job and want to do your best. Maybe part of your duties is organising an annual staff conference. It's a ton of extra work, but everybody looks forward to it every year and it's been a runaway success. You feel like the conference is essential, but is it? Is it critical for the organisation's growth? Of course, it's nice to make people feel happy and everyone loves the nice photos on the company's Insta feed, but what's strategic about it?

There may be another way to think about this, but you won't know unless you seek other opinions. If you do, someone may point out that while the retreat is popular and well-received, it's not popular because it feeds directly into making work work for everyone. There's the cost of having hundreds of people away for the day. Is that good for the bottom line of the business? Are you really getting good ROI? The conference really only focuses on business updates—how is each team going to contribute to the strategy for the year, but maybe these can be delivered in another format or through another channel that eats up less of your time and resources. Could a 'conference' of sorts still provide connection, include play with purpose and also double down on value? In looking at it this way—by getting that new point of view—you might see that the retreat is unnecessary and remove it from the following year's calendar. This frees up your time and lightens your heavy workload. With the extra time, it might be possible to create an initiative that takes less of your time but is still popular AND adds value to the organisation.

I talk about conversations in other parts of this book, and quality conversations are at the centre of good coaching. We all have biases and filters in the way we see things, just like we were divided on the colour of that dress. No single person can see the full picture. But in a frank and open heart-to-heart, peers can learn from each other's point of view. This starts by seeking someone's perspective and considering it. Then you can reflect on and expand your own point of view. It's not necessarily about challenging another person's opinions. It's not about who is right and who is wrong. As assumptions are tested and more deeply understood, new insights and ideas can be uncovered. The process is iterative. Peers come together to collectively consider an issue, with trust at the centre. Over time, we build bigger and more complex perspectives and viewpoints that help us see challenges differently and discover more potential solutions. Research supports this. Peer coaching has been shown to accelerate organisational change and create a self-sustaining coaching organisation.[31]

In terms of coaching, this is reciprocal. When different perspectives are shared, the views of both participants can be changed. When coaching is done well, both the coach and the coachee learn about themselves, and this leads to growth. When peer-to-peer coaching is embedded in an organisation, the whole organisation grows. When good coaching happens at more senior levels, where there is more connectivity and power, the depth and breadth of change is exponential. Ripples are felt to the very edges of the organisation. Leaders cast long shadows—small movements by a leader become large movements at the end of the shadow.

I want to be crystal clear here. This is about more than seeing somebody else's point of view. It's about more than walking a mile in someone else's shoes. When two perspectives are on the table, you can choose one or the other. Or even better, further perspectives can emerge.

My view + Your view = Bigger view + Something new.

---

31 Ladyshewsky, R., & Taplin, R. (2017). Employee perceptions of managerial coaching and work engagement using the Measurement Model of Coaching Skills and the Utrecht Work Engagement Scale. *International Journal of Evidence Based Coaching and Mentoring, 15*(2), 25–42.

Here's a visual to show you what I mean. I call it 'Options vs. Insights: the Growth Line'. As you can see, the Y-axis shows the insights gained and is about how much you see. The X-axis shows the volume of solutions and options. The rising line shows how potential options expand as more insights are sought.

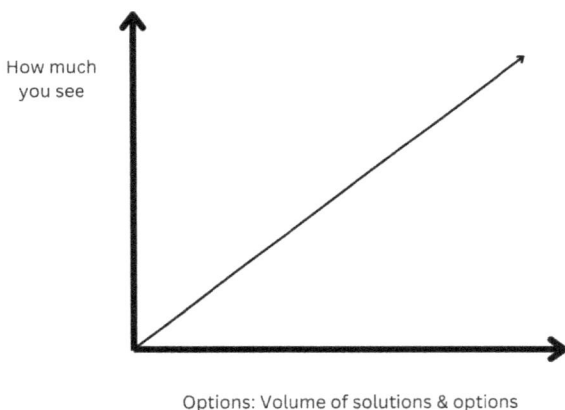

Options: Volume of solutions & options

FIGURE 23 Options vs Insights: The Growth Line

You might have to wait a while for the payoff. Think of mortgage brokers who get upfront payments but have to wait for the commissions. Those commissions are like the 'something new' that's born from the union of different perspectives, the growth that happens when you seek other people's views and hold them and integrate them over time. Be patient; you will get better and achieve more.

This might not be easy, but it's important. Leaders and organisations can get better at leading change, managing performance, catalysing a team, creating a compelling vision and seeing the broader context when they're ready, willing and able to add their view to other views to create a bigger view and something new. Being able to gather and see many points of view, put them out on the table to see and work with them, even combine them, is one of the ways to create effective behaviour change.[32]

The research supports this. A study by Latorre et al. (2020) found that perspective-taking capacity in leaders is positively correlated with team performance and job satisfaction. Research by Galinsky and Moskowitz (2000) indicates that perspective taking leads to improved negotiation outcomes and conflict resolution. Organisations become more effective and adaptive in response to complexity, uncertainty and continuous change. All of this fuels growth and helps the organisation to get better.

Making it work

When it comes to embedding peer-to-peer coaching, it doesn't have to be a formal, programmatic thing that creates a logistical nightmare and a lot of work. Start small. And remember that peers do not have to be from the same department. One can be from technology, the other from sales. Get views

---

32 https://www.mckinsey.com/featured-insights/leadership/change-leader-change-thyself

from people who don't have the same background as you. Deliberately seek out difference.

If you already reach out to peers, great. I suggest the conversation changes from: 'Hey, can I get your perspective… How do you see this situation…' to one where you share your views on something. When peers listen and ask questions, using their own perspective, both parties help to illuminate the picture. You'll see more and see challenges in a whole new way, which gives you more options for change. It's through taking on experiences in the throes of work that new neural pathways are built. That growth will enable increases in performance. That's how I design my programs, and if we end up working together we'll extend on this work. But for now, you can do some DIY coaching to illuminate peer perspectives to solve problems and grow.

But before you get started, I want you to do a self-check. I'm sure you know people who are just so stuck in their ways. It's their way or the highway. They believe that nonsense about teaching an old dog new tricks. They don't have it in them to see another side of the story… don't have the capacity. As a leader in this complex world, you cannot afford to be one of them. But how do you know if you're in that category? Can you be sure you don't have any blind spots? Just like changing lanes when you're driving, you need to look over your shoulder to take in the whole view. So let's turn the mirror on you and see what blind spots might be obstructing your growth, how you grow others and how you lead change in your organisation. If you're going to coach your peers and *be coached by them*, you need to be open to the new insights and views that this practice creates. You yourself must be coachable.

I call this exercise 'Gauge your growth: Are you ready to roll?'

Consider the following statements, which are drawn from comic strips, memes and various unknown sources. Do they resonate? Do you laugh with guilt when you read them?

❑ 'I don't need to walk in your shoes; mine are more comfortable.'

❑ 'If I wanted your opinion, I'd give it to you.'

❑ 'Why ask for input when you already have the answer?'

If you answered 'yes' to any, some or all of these, you may not be willing to 'give it a go'.

❑ 'I asked for feedback. It was just for show.'

❑ 'I listen to everyone. Then I make the right decision—mine.'

❑ 'I love asking for advice. Just so I can ignore it.'

❑ 'I asked for your opinion, not because I need it, but because I needed to confirm mine.'

If you answered 'yes' to any, some or all of these, you may not be willing to 'branch out'.

- ❏ 'I'm open to new ideas, as long as they're mine.'

- ❏ 'I take everyone's opinion into account. Then I do what I wanted to do in the first place.'

- ❏ 'My favourite kind of opinion is one that agrees with mine.'

- ❏ 'I'm not ignoring you; I'm just filtering out the noise.'

- ❏ 'I accept all opinions, but I only respect mine.'

If you answered 'yes' to any, some or all of these, you may not be open minded.

- ❏ I'm curious about your thoughts … so I can correct them.'

- ❏ 'Tell me your opinion so I can dismantle it.'

- ❏ 'Tell me more so I can tell you why you're wrong.'

- ❏ 'I'm asking questions to understand where you went wrong.'

If you answered 'yes' to any, some or all of these, you may not understand the thinking behind people's points of view.

- ☐ 'I respect your right to be wrong.'

- ☐ 'I hear what you're saying, but it's wrong.'

- ☐ 'My opinion isn't the only one, it's just the right one.'

If you answered 'yes' to any, some or all of these, you may not believe other points of view are valid. Your thinking may be black and white.

Coaching accelerates growth. When your organisation needs to put its foot on the growth pedal, peer-to-peer coaching is a relatively easy practice to embed in a non-programmatic way. It won't happen overnight, as they say in the shampoo world, but you're intentional about this, remain patient and keep your mind open. Guided growth will help to make work work for you.

ORGANISATION PERFORMANCE

TAKE OFF AND TRANSFORM

*Transform and take off: Drive performance
with More speed, less waste and fast learning.*

HAVE YOU ever been close to a kangaroo bounding
across a paddock? Sadly, I haven't, but people have
told me that when you're close, you can actually
feel the vibration passing through the ground and
into your feet as the mob's collective hind legs hit
the ground before they take off. And it is like taking
off. They don't really jump. Or even hop. They just
sort of effortlessly rise into the air. The secret lies
in their powerful hind legs, which store mechanical
energy in the tendons during each jump. That stored
energy is what allows them to rebound so effortlessly. They're fast f***ers, too. There's a good reason
for those road signs asking motorists to watch out
for kangaroos: they can reach speeds of sixty kilometres an hour, and the big reds can jump as high

as three metres and as far as seven metres in a single jump.

Now, I'm taking a leap here[33], but I think high-performing organisations are a bit like kangaroos. They're both alive, at least in the sense that they use energy, grow and develop, and have to respond to the environment to survive. Like a kangaroo leaping past a car flying down the highway, speed is a key to survival. If an organisation isn't ready to pounce, they'll miss out. Just like a kangaroo, more speed, less waste and fast learning (a.k.a. an effortless rebound) are what a business needs to survive.

I'm talking about agility here, of course. Since the Agile Manifesto was published in 2001, this way of working has spread beyond the original software development space and begun to permeate more and more industries and applications. There are Agile project teams, Agile ways of working and Agile maturity assessments. There are WAgile projects that combine both the Agile and Waterfall methodologies. More and more organisations are calling themselves Agile. Others are being born Agile. In fact, there's so much 'agile' stuff going on that people are getting confused and the term has even become a bit 'cringe'. But Agile with a capital 'A' is not what I'm talking about here. Some reframing is required.

The last thing I want to give you is a manifesto. A prescriptive list of methodologies is the opposite of 'agility'. But you do need agility in the modern

---

33 Pun intended!

marketplace. I've spent decades working with companies on change initiatives. When you need to give that performance pedal a nudge, you need to lean into agility, particularly that fast learning and rebound. It should be part of your muscle memory. But are you bringing an agile mindset? Are you actually doing it? I want this to be a reminder for you, a prompt to check yourself to make sure you're using your agility.

Revving up performance is about failing fast, sharing early and growing early. It's about hitting the ground running with a new idea and leaping in headfirst. It's about going to market with a description and product catalogue without having built the prototype. You need to put things out there with an authentic learning mindset to see what sticks. This is the approach that characterises the start-up world, where I've spent a large part of my career in change management and learnt a lot.

I knew the COO of a medium-sized company who came up with the idea for a huge roadshow in the morning and had it out to market by the afternoon—it was on the website, and they were advertising and testing to gauge customer interest before planning out a single detail. The idea was to get a waiting list of people willing to buy a ticket before they took it any further.

I understand that some people think this type of approach is backwards. Others find it too uncomfortable to consider. For others, this approach just doesn't show up on their radar. But I prefer to think of it as three steps forward and two steps back.

Head off in what you think is the right direction, but course-correct as soon as you spot an obstacle, just like a kangaroo drawing on all that energy stored in their tendons. You might slip back a bit, but you have still made ground. And if you make like a kangaroo, your rebound will be graceful and effortless.

I get that this is hard to do, so let's consider some of the obstacles to agility.

Perfectionism? Overrated.

You might want that document to look perfect and professional. Fair enough—some people are so distracted by the poor look and feel of a document they can't see the content printed on it. But just how perfect does it have to be? You need a minimum viable product, that's all. Yes, it must be legible, but it doesn't need to be perfectly bound. A staple in the corner may be enough.

Wedded to one particular outcome? File for divorce. There are many ways to achieve a result, so get busy on the metaphorical dating scene before committing. Clear your mind and listen to people's opinions. Take in the data; don't impose your own thoughts. Let that fuel the cycle of change. Dare I say—embrace the journey?

Fear of failure? What failure? It's called learning. Be brave enough to ask for feedback before the draft is ready. If the tone or content is wrong, you need that early intervention to save precious time and resources.

An organisation must be ready to respond and react when new opportunities come along. If you're not ready to pounce, you'll miss out. If you move too slowly to develop a new product, it can be out of date by the time it hits the market. Do I really need to say 'Edsall'?

When your company is agile, flexible and nimble, people expect the business to keep moving. Dynamism is built in. This helps create accountability because people need to know the status of every project. There's an impetus to keep on top of things. All of this keeps that performance pedal revving.

I've lost count of the number of leaders I've coached in this space. And I don't want to teach grandma to suck eggs. I know you understand the mindset and mechanics of agility. But are you actually doing it? Are you personally enhancing the whole organisation's ability to be agile? Being comfortable with imperfection can expose vulnerabilities. How will you create a safe place for this to happen? You need trust from all corners to support agility. Leaders must set an example and create the conditions. What are you enabling—overtly or otherwise? What's your response when someone comes to you with a half-baked idea?

Making it work

It's time to take a look at your organisation to figure out if you have the speed, efficiency and rebound ability you need to survive. What's the musculoskeletal system of your organisation look like? What strengths will power you to leap ahead? What's in place to enable balance, support and speed in an efficient and sustainable way? Let's have a look at a visual to help us understand this. I call this the 'Quick Leap Model'.

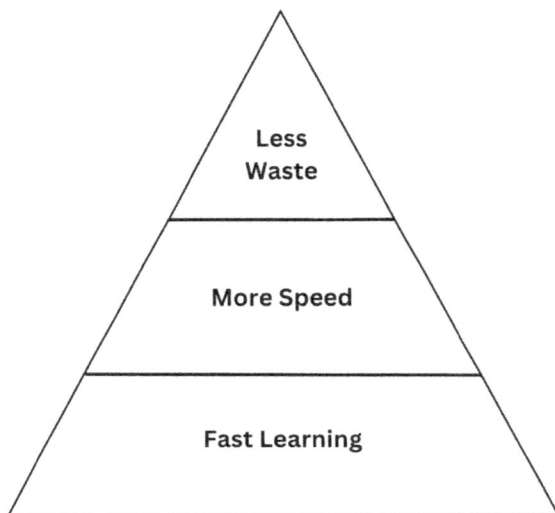

FIGURE 24 Quick Leap Model

First, ask yourself: How fast can you go from idea to putting a product to market to test so you can learn and iterate?

At the height of COVID-19, I was concerned about what would happen between people, including my young kids, if they couldn't see my facial cues. I teamed up with a former colleague and entrepreneur and tried to solve that problem by introducing clear face masks. We did this quickly by chatting to our friends and anyone and everyone we ran into. It was energising to talk to people like local baristas, who were also concerned and wanted a clear mask.

The former colleague I was working with wanted to go from identifying a problem to putting out a potential solution for testing or validation over a single weekend. On the Friday we identified the pain point: masks that got in the way of seeing a person's reaction. By Monday the website was up and running, showing mock-ups of clear masks and asking people to register their interest.

My mate was an entrepreneur and knew that speed to market was everything. Going from idea to taking it to market in a single weekend is what I mean by speed. Can your organisation do that? Are you pressing hard enough on that performance pedal?

Next, ask yourself: How much waste are you creating when you test a new idea? How scrappy can you be to learn what you need to learn so you can grow and survive (a.k.a. bring in the money)? In bootstrapping start-ups, this is everything.

I once had the bright idea to create a loneliness program. The data, which was certainly there, told me there are a lot of lonely hearts beating quietly by themselves, yearning for connection and friendship. No worries, I thought, I'll create a loneliness program, and all the lonely people can join it and make heartwarming connections with each other. The result when I went to market? Nothing. Nada. Turns out, people who are lonely aren't keen on joining a loneliness program. Duh!

But I wasn't discouraged. My MVP was minimal—a single PowerPoint slide. So not much time and effort wasted there. Obviously I had to pivot, but it was no elephant stomp. By not being overly attached to an outcome, I was able to let go before my idea dragged me down with it. I managed a graceful, roo-like rebound and simply repackaged the program as building meaningful connections. And it worked! The program was a great success. Turns out lonely people don't want to sign up for programs for lonely people. But they did want to build meaningful connections with people around them.

Finally, ask yourself: How quickly can you cull and kill ideas? How quickly can you learn and bounce away from danger, just like a kangaroo?

On a family holiday in Fiji, my frozen mango daiquiris were served with a green straw. It wasn't metal, it wasn't plastic and it wasn't paper... turns out it was made from an edible material that fish could eat if it found its way into the ocean. Completely biodegradable. Better drinking experience, better for the environment, win-win.

I was so excited by this idea that I couldn't sleep and sat up in bed, taking lots of notes on my phone about the worldwide problem with straws. The sogginess of the paper... The inconvenience of the metal alternative... I brainstormed the business model, how I'd get clients, resources I'd need, everything. I was filling out a business model canvas in my head.

But one thing I've learnt through my entrepreneurship training, and in practice, is that all hypotheses need testing. And if you want to learn fast, you need to find the quickest and easiest way to prove an idea is a s*** idea that's not worth pursuing.

So I spoke to my dad, a retired business owner who used to have a B2B business in engineering, working with products with a low price point in high volumes (similar to the straw business idea in many ways). He thought it was good, but we weren't sure if the numbers and small margins would stack up.

Next I called a friend who's a business owner. 'Hey Liam, I have another idea. I need it gone from my mind or I need to move forward and do something with it, can you help me kill it?" We killed it in less than five minutes.

Not all decisions should be made this quickly, but the start-up world taught me when to nuke an idea so I can bounce swiftly away and move on to the next potential genius idea. And it's important to note that this doesn't just apply to products. It can be applied to lots of things like sharing and validating ideas between teams. Whether it's a product, a service or just an idea, if something isn't going to work, you want to know that ASAP so you can either kill it fast or get it out fast so you can learn fast.

To test how agile your organisation is, I've devised a scoring system called the Kangaroo—Sloth Agility Self-Check. Just like that kangaroo taking off, agility is all about fast learning, more speed and less waste. This exercise will establish whether you're a slow-moving sloth or a kangaroo capable of making leaps and bounds.

For each statement below, rate yourself (I) and your organisation (We) on a scale from 1 to 5, where 1 is 'Not at all' and 5 is 'Absolutely'.

Exercise: Kangaroo—Sloth Agility Self-Check

1: Fast Learning

I/We learn quickly from each hop, adjusting our course when needed.

——— 1   2   3   4   5 ——→

I/We pivot fast when a leap doesn't go as planned, just like a roo changing direction mid-jump.

——— 1   2   3   4   5 ——→

I/We encourage trying new paths, even if it means a few stumbles along the way.

——— 1   2   3   4   5 ——→

2: More Speed

I/We can leap from idea to action with ease.

———— 1   2   3   4   5 ———→

My/Our decision-making process is quick and nimble, like a kangaroo's reflexes.

———— 1   2   3   4   5 ———→

I/We have the speed to take new ideas to market before the competition catches up.

———— 1   2   3   4   5 ———→

3: Less Waste

I/We keep our jumps efficient, using just the right amount of energy to get where we need to go.

———— 1   2   3   4   5 ———→

My/Our processes are streamlined, avoiding unnecessary hops and skips.

———— 1   2   3   4   5 ———→

I/We allocate resources wisely, so nothing gets wasted on fruitless leaps.

———— 1   2   3   4   5 ———→

Assess the Gap

1   How agile do I/we need to be to stay ahead of the pack?

- No change needed.
- Slight improvement needed.
- Big leaps needed.

2   What's the biggest gap between where we are and where we need to be?

- Fast learning
- More speed
- Less waste

Reflection

- Did your ratings differ when thinking about yourself (I) vs. your organisation ('We)? If so, where's the disconnect?

- What's one small step you could take to help your team or organisation hop to it?

More speed, less waste and fast learning are hallmarks of the start-up, but all organisations need the ability to lean into these qualities. Today's market conditions and organisations are undergoing continual changes. Agility, adaptability and flexibility are becoming increasingly important to management performance.[34] When organisational performance

---

34   Kenneth P. De Meuse, Guangrong Dai, and George S. Hallenbeck. Learning agility: A construct whose time has come. *Consulting Psychology Journal: Practice and Research.* 2010, Vol. 62, No. 2, 119–130

is flagging and you need to hit that pedal and rev things up, take a look at how these qualities show up. A tweak in this direction may be what you need to bound towards excellence and get work working for you.

CULTIVATE
YOUR CULTURE

Culture is co-created, not commanded:
Leaders and teams shape culture together
through intentional practices.

TO HELP you understand culture, let me invite you to a party...

The theme is Miami Vice. Your invitation contained a fake tattoo of the birthday boy in a pastel pink shirt and blazer. You smile as you apply it before donning your costume. The look you're going for is undercover detective on the streets of Miami, circa 1980s. It gets you in the mood. When you rock up to the house, you can hear the beat of the music, signalling a fun night ahead. Red carpet has been laid in the driveway. The birthday boy's daughter has been cast as photographer for the night. She gets right into her role, snapping and flashing and getting in your face like a real paparazzo. You don your Ray-Bans and roll up onto the red carpet laid on the driveway. A borrowed Ferrari is parked at a nonchalant angle, and you're handed a peach-coloured cocktail as you step through to the backyard and take in the scene. Everyone has entered into the spirit. Costumes are so imaginative you can hardly recognise your friends in their wigs and shades and shoulder pads. Blow-up pink flamingos are bobbing in the swimming pool. The buzz is infectious. You're in for a fun night.

Now, you can't order people to have fun. But you can create the right conditions for the fun to emerge organically. The party organiser has a responsibility here. They must create the right atmosphere by choosing the right theme, the right music and the right food. Guests have a role to play too. My best friend's mum used to say, when she drove us to parties when we were moody, uncooperative teenagers, 'Be a good party guest!' At a good party, everyone contributes. There's a sense of generosity. All the guests get into the spirit of things. There's a commitment. And this is easier when the host creates fertile conditions for the fun to grow naturally and vigorously.

At a good party, the vibe evolves as the night rolls on, and everyone picks up on the unwritten rules. In my metaphorical party, there are young children sleeping upstairs, so that area is off limits. Not because there's a security guard standing on the landing with arms crossed, looking threatening, but because everybody takes the right cues from each other about what's appropriate. It's like this in the workplace too—rules of engagement exist, but they're usually implicit. Environment shapes behaviour; we know that. People are more likely to litter when there's litter lying around.

So you see the point I'm making. The vibe—at either a party or in a workplace—emerges naturally and is influenced by the conditions. It can't be forced. And it's co-created by the host and the guests or the leader and their team—both influence the culture. But who is the most important person? At the party, it's the birthday boy, of course, and in the workplace it's the leader.

Employees look to the leader and ask themselves, 'What does this person want to see from me?' Whether consciously or unconsciously, the leader signals the answer to this unspoken question. The cues and clues are noticed. People catch a whiff of these things. And it's as much about what people *don't* do as what they *do* do.

Let's clarify by looking at two approaches to the same situation and how that plays out as culture. In Company A, when somebody misses a deadline, it might be acceptable to call it out and discuss the issue in a meeting so that everyone's clear on what the expectations are. But in Company B, the employee responsible for missing the deadline will be quietly pulled aside for a one-on-one conversation. They'll be asked the reasons for the missed deadline and what support they need for future tasks. Neither approach is inherently right or wrong, but both are symbols of the culture and, therefore, provide clues to what the vibe is. This is how culture is expressed, absorbed and embodied.

So why is it important to have the 'right' culture? Because the wrong culture will send value flying out the door as employees leave for a better workplace. The right culture is the one that's going to enable the organisation to perform and achieve its strategy.

Good culture attracts good talent, and it also helps to retain it. People come to work for many reasons—work can be a job, a career or a calling—but almost everyone stays for the same reason. That reason is the team. People stay for the team they're in and leave for the team they're not in. People stay for the community. The community embodies the culture.

I recently joined a group of fellow business owners to help me grow my business and learn. I did grow my business and I did learn, but I've stayed for the community. People take out memberships for co-working spaces so they can have a desk outside their homes, but they stay for the vibe and the salty margaritas. How many times have you heard someone complain about difficult clients and asked why they don't look for work somewhere else? The answer is always the same: 'I love my team and the people I work with.' This is good culture.

It can be hard for a leader to let workplace culture emerge and evolve. Leaders want control, but if your employees say they need more fun in the workplace, you can't command them to have fun.

Culture can't be controlled because it's not a cult. Thank God—because cults don't work. You can't make fun of an agenda item (even though I've seen this happen). The fun emerges in the right conditions. So create those conditions—just like a savvy gardener prepares the soil before planting a tree to give it the best start in life.

Making it work

First you must decide what you want the culture to be. There's some design required here; you may want to nudge the culture in a certain direction. For example, is the culture currently too nice? Perhaps you want a culture that makes it possible—safe—to lean into difficult conversations. I was brought in to work with some leaders who all liked each other, but because of this, no one gave anyone feedback. They saw each other as friends and didn't want to risk upsetting their relationships.

Once you've decided on the culture you want, put practices in place that allow it to emerge. To show you exactly what I mean, let's look at some hypothetical examples...

Say you want to normalise failure in your organisation. This is common in start-ups; if you're not failing, you're not learning. One way to do this is to organise 'f***-up nights'. Get everybody together where there's a stage, or improvise a stage in the tearoom or boardroom. Then hand the mic to the first brave or reckless volunteer and ask them to let loose with a story about a time they—well—f***ed-up. Don't ask for a sober and reflective account of grave lessons learnt from mistakes; ask the speaker to tell their story of failure in all its inglorious detail. Then ask everybody in the audience to give them a vigorous round of applause. Perhaps even a standing ovation. After a few hilarious sessions, failure will begin to normalise and become an acceptable part of the culture.

Another example could be the need for a culture that's hyper customer-centric, where employees are obsessive about making everything about the customer. This could be the case in a company that, say, manufactures fresh food kits or ready meals. The food can be served in the company canteen or cafeteria, which gives employees a chance to taste it. And not just the chefs or the salespeople, but the forklift drivers and the accountants and the C-suite executives. Every employee can eat it for lunch, take it home to their families for dinner, share it with the neighbours and put this sumptuous food at the centre of their lives. They'll learn to love it and become raving fans. They'll experience the company's products just as the customers do, almost becoming proxies for the customers. What better way to ensure everybody in the company is thinking of the customer?

Culture is about energy, about the buzz of the team. It can't be prescribed, but it can be encouraged to grow by creating the right environment. By designing and embedding imaginative practices into the organisation's routines, you create the conditions that send the right message about 'how things are done around here'.

If you think you need to cultivate your culture more intentionally, reflect on these questions and think about how your actions (or inactions) contribute to creating the right conditions—like the perfect temperature for yoghurt to grow its good bacteria—where your ideal culture can develop. Consider whether your current culture is 'set' the way your organisation truly needs.

- How do we celebrate success?
- What happens when someone makes a mistake?
- How do we handle conflicts and disagreements?

Having the right culture in your organisation will fuel your performance. It's not an obvious route to improved performance, but when the vibe is right and people stay for the atmosphere, the work works for everyone. If you need to get some revs on the performance pedal, try tweaking your culture. Before you know it, you'll be doing great.

MINE SOME METAPHORS

Go beyond convention: Use creative metaphors to unlock your thinking and boost performance.

DID YOU KNOW that proofreaders don't just read a book from start to finish and correct the typos and errors they find? The proofreader for my book will certainly do this, but my editor told me something fascinating about how she will do it. Proofreading, I learnt, is more than reading. It's the art of seeing. Our eyes tend not to notice all the errors in text because our brain automatically corrects them. It's possible to read quite fluently when only the first and last letters of the words are visible; our brains simply fill in the blanks. That's why proofreading is difficult—mistakes are elusive. A good proofreader will not just read the words; she will look at the shape of the letters. Reading the book backwards, paragraph by paragraph is another proofreading technique that helps keep the brain alert to errors that might otherwise be hiding. Even more fascinating is that a good proofreader will proofread not just the words but the white space. Looking at the white space and how it holds the words on the page can reveal otherwise invisible errors.

Looking at things in a different way—finding a new way to see something familiar—is essential for creativity. The paragraph you just read was a metaphor that helped to explain that concept. It's common to use metaphors to communicate. Most of us do this all the time. Some oldies but goodies: 'time is money', 'climb the ladder', 'think outside the box', 'low-hanging fruit', 'breaking down siloes', 'putting out fires', 'running around like a headless chook'. Metaphors help us get a point across.

I love metaphors, similes and analogies (and I'm really talking about all three here). They pop out of me all the time. My editor played a game of whack-a-mole with me as she tried to stop them from shooting out of every pore on my body. Again and again, she told me: 'Metaphors are great for helping to explain a new concept, but they are not the concept itself!' But this time they are... prepare yourself for a wild ride.

My editor was right when she said that metaphors are a great way to explain a concept—these are called 'explanatory' metaphors and they do just that—clarify, explain or illustrate complex ideas by relating them to something more familiar. The common examples I listed above are explanatory metaphors. But there is also something called the 'exploratory' metaphor. This is where things get exciting, where we have an opportunity to use metaphors in how we think and how we solve problems. Metaphors engage what's called 'meta-thinking', where people reflect on their thinking processes and perceive complex relationships among seemingly unrelated concepts. Doing this allows them to solve problems in innovative ways by using metaphors, analogies and abstract thinking to make connections that might otherwise remain unseen. Metaphors are creative portals that build bridges between seemingly unrelated thoughts.

The purpose of an exploratory metaphor (or simile or analogy) is to explore an idea, provoke thought or encourage new insights and perspectives. It's a tool that can help you to think more deeply and broadly, leading to new interpretations or discoveries. A common example of an exploratory metaphor could be thinking about life as a journey. This invites you to think about life in terms of exploration, progress and personal growth. This could lead to various interpretations of experiences, goals and challenges. Unlike explanatory metaphors, which aim to make concepts clear, exploratory metaphors are thought-provoking. Explanatory metaphors are useful in teaching and instruction—you've probably noticed that I've used them a lot in that way in this book. Exploratory metaphors are used in creative writing, discussions and brainstorming sessions.

This is why I'm introducing you to them—they're rocket fuel for creativity and innovation.

Exploratory metaphors encourage thinking beyond conventional boundaries by drawing comparisons between unrelated experiences. They encourage new perspectives by helping you see problems and solutions from different angles. They stimulate imaginative thinking and help you break free from linear and routine patterns. They can also create a common language for complex ideas, which makes it easier for teams to share and develop innovative concepts. They provoke thought by prompting deeper reflection on existing processes and systems, which leads to new insights and ideas.

So that's the theory; time for an example. Let's start with shoes. We want a shoe to be strong yet lightweight. What's out there in the world that's like that? Hmmm... A spiderweb! How can we apply the metaphor of a spiderweb to shoe manufacturing? Maybe that's what the brains at Nike were thinking when they developed their Flyknit technology, which digitally knits the entire upper part of the shoe in one piece to make it strong, yet lightweight. This new tech led to material savings and a revolution in shoe manufacturing.

Now let's consider cars. We want a car that's like a horse; it knows when to speed up and when to stop. What is it about a horse that can be applied to the car? It takes cues from its environment and can make decisions based on those cues, just like a living thing with a brain. It's said that Google's driverless car project was propelled by this metaphor.

Here's an example from my own life... I like to take my kids to Yo-Chi, the self-serve frozen yoghurt shop. It's not cheap—$25 for two tubs of yoghurt and toppings, but it's packed out in summer. So what's their secret? It's on trend with a very clear target audience of young adults and parents with young kids. It's an experience, too. There's a particular vibe with the music and décor. What else? People like the autonomy of serving themselves. They like the choice of flavours. And even though the selection isn't large, customers can mix and match. Anyway, one day while I was helping the kids fill up their tubs, I used Yo-Chi as a metaphor and applied it to my own business. How many flavours did I have? What was on the menu? Actually, I didn't have a menu. That's when it clicked. Creating a menu of standard services would make it easier for people to buy from me. Bam! Metaphor magic...

Making it work

So how do you start using metaphors in your business to foster creativity? First you must expose yourself to metaphors. You need to think of some before you start using them for exploration and creativity. You could certainly buy or borrow a book of metaphors—such books exist—but at the most basic level finding metaphors simply involves living your life and keeping your mind open. When I read—fiction, non-fiction, blog posts, whatever—if something resonates it goes into Evernote and I tag it. I might not know why it's resonating, but this gives me a bunch of concepts that I might be able to use later to fuel my creative thinking. Being open minded is how I arrived at the menu idea for my business when I visited Yo-Chi.

Open your eyes and look around. Is there something in the garden that you can relate to a work problem? Maybe the lemon tree is heavy with ripe fruit that's out of reach. You need a ladder to get to the lemons on the higher branches before they drop on the ground and rot. Are your salespeople able to get to out-of-reach prospects? Do they need a metaphorical ladder? What might that be? You've no doubt heard of the 'low-hanging' fruit metaphor to describe prospects that are easy to convert. See how you're already using metaphors? Another to consider… Can the jumble of magnets on the fridge door help you improve logistics? When you tidy up the magnets, does a surprising structure emerge? Do they fit together in unexpected ways? Are there similar, surprising ways of linking elements in your supply chain?

Using metaphors to improve creativity can be fun but is also a challenge when it's new. To help you get started, I've designed a process I call the 'Metaphor-Driven Creativity Approach'. Here are the steps:

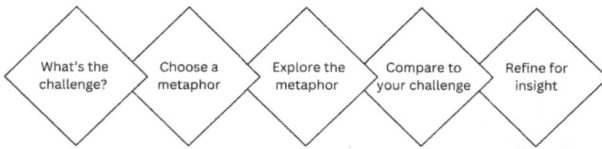

FIGURE 25 Metaphor-Driven Creativity Approach

Now let's go through it together using a real-world example...

I worked with a leader once whose challenge was the need to boost sales (step 1).

I chose the metaphor of fishing to help him deal with the challenge (step 2).

In exploring the metaphor (step 3), he had various thoughts. When you fish, you catch more when you've got the right bait, when you're in the right spot, when the conditions are right, and if you've got a net or a fish finder.[35] If you're not fussy about what you catch and have to throw back, you'll have more fish in your bag at the end of the day. If you go with a friend you'll catch more. If you have more time with your rod in the water, you'll catch more, and so on.

In comparing the metaphor to the challenge (step 4), we analysed the 'bait' (promotions/discounts/incentives/brand) to see how he could attract more customers. Was he in the right spot to attract more

---

35 A fish finder is a device that detects schools of fish by transmitting ultrasonic waves into the sea and receiving their reflection.

customers (targeting the right customer demographic, etc.).

Then the leader had an 'aha' moment. The team didn't have a 'fish finder'. This was the real insight, and at this point, the leader was able to stop using the metaphor because he had helpful insight to act on. That is, how could he get more data to help him work out where to find more clients and, therefore, boost sales, which was the original challenge.

Learning the 'Metaphor-Driven Creativity Approach' is one thing, but to truly embed this process, you need to follow three ongoing practices that sit around it.

1 **Create that white space**. Intentionally find information and inspiration from the environment that's beyond the boundary of the office building and desk.

2 **Lift up and look out**. As a deliberate practice, notice things in detail and generate insight. Deliberately examine things you find when you 'lift up and look out'. Bank them in your memory.

3 **Inject innovation**. Use the above steps and combine them with areas of focus, the problem to be solved, the goal to be reached, where that injection of innovation is needed. This is where the Metaphor-Driven Creativity Approach is powerful.

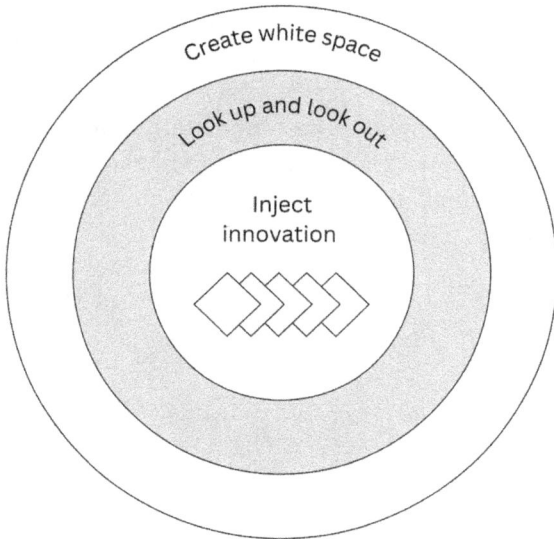

FIGURE 26 White Space Framework for Strategic Innovation

Using metaphors to foster creativity is like travelling. If you're feeling stale, you might need to get out more—travel to exotic places and see the many wonders of the world. There are some jaw-dropping places to see and experiences to have on planet Earth. Be curious about what you see; ask questions and make comparisons. Travel is a way to discover and uncover new insights, ideas and inspiration. And if you can't get away from your desk to travel in time and space, let your mind wander and find new associations between the elements of your life. Then apply those associations to your business problems.

And yes, that was a metaphor about metaphors...

Using exploratory metaphors to solve business challenges is not easy. It's challenging and requires sophisticated thinking. But it's also a press on that performance pedal that other leaders may not be doing. To move your organisation further down the road of excellence, I recommend you start mining some metaphors.

CONCLUSION
MAKE WORK WORK FOR YOU
NOW AND IN THE FUTURE

WE'RE IN a moment when rethinking work is more important than ever. The need to make work truly work for more people is urgent. In this book, we've explored twenty-seven leadership practices aimed at boosting performance, growth and wellbeing. But our mission doesn't end here. The world of work is changing fast, and so must we.

We're seeing people move away from traditional jobs, with more turning to the gig economy. Tech advancements are automating routine tasks. More people are being identified as neurodivergent later in life. These shifts are shaking up who works, how they work, and what work means.

As tech handles the mundane work, creativity and human skills are becoming more critical. And it's clear that sticking to old ways of thinking won't cut it. Like Einstein said, 'We cannot solve our problems with the same thinking we used when we created them.' We need to evolve—not just in our organisations, but in ourselves.

It's time that we step up and create a transformation—these global shifts demand it. Robert Kegan talked about the need for transformation back in 1994, pointing out that we're often 'in over our heads'—and that's even more true today. His work on adult development shows that personal growth is ongoing, and it's something leaders and organisations need to embrace to create excellence in today's complex, fluid world of work.

But this transformation isn't just about embracing new tech or processes. It's about creating spaces where people can genuinely be themselves. Yes, there's tension here. While many organisations say they want people to bring their authentic selves to work, they're often not ready to handle the diversity of thought and needs that come with this—especially when it comes to neurodivergent individuals. Bridging this gap is crucial if we're serious about making work work for everyone.

Success in the future of work isn't about doing more of the same. The definition of success is shifting from traditional metrics to a more balanced approach that values purpose and meaning as well as performance. As we strive for excellence, we've got to make sure we're not burning out on the way. The three pedals of excellence—performance, growth, and wellbeing—need to stay in balance and fuel each other for sustainable success.

In a world that's changing faster than ever, the time to act is now. Like Moloko's song says, 'The time is now.' We can't afford to wait. We need to lead the change, driving forward with a relentless focus on making work work for everyone.

The future of work is about more than keeping up with change; it's about shaping it. Leaders who get this will both handle the challenges ahead and seize the opportunities that come with them. As we close this book and look to the future, let's commit to continuous learning, to transforming ourselves and our organisations, and to making work work— for everyone, now and in the future.

I have more resources for you to help you shape change.

.

NEXT
STEPS

SO, YOU HAVE read the book, now what?

You understand what it means to make work work for you, but we all know it's not enough to just read the book. It's the actions you take next that really matter.

You know that to make change happen, you must do something. The something I am suggesting you do now is take some steps towards a better work life, greater wellbeing, or reaching even higher performance—and that means putting what you have read into practice.

So, start small. Start tiny. I suggest you **choose one practice at a time**, put it into action, come back and then move on to the next.

Remember, the book has been designed so you can pick it up, put it down, practise one practice and then pick it up again.

My hope is this book will be a catalyst to effect real change in your life or perhaps—for those of you who have known for a while you needed to change your relationship to your work—it will motivate you to take action now.

I'd like to keep supporting you to change, so I've put together a special bonus to help you achieve just that!

Go to https://louise-gilbert.com/book-bonus-tools/ and download your free bonus tools. These tools are designed to be super practical, and easy to use.

I want to ensure you get the most out of the time you have spent reading and this is my way of also saying thanks for buying my book!

SCAN FOR YOUR BONUS TOOLS

ABOUT
LOUISE GILBERT

The author, Louise Gilbert, is the Director of the business by the same name: *Louise Gilbert.*

LOUISE GILBERT has grown significantly in the past five years, having advised some of Australia's top leaders and organisations to manage change and guided teams to achieve business excellence.

The company offers a wide range of services to businesses large and small, including change and leadership coaching; facilitating real shifts in team and leadership dynamics; workshops and advice on developing high-performing teams; consulting services; keynote speeches; and specialist training. All programs are 100% tailored based on a full understanding of the organisation's and team's unique challenges.

Utilising the proven model of the 'three pedals of excellence' many of *Louise Gilbert's* clients have experienced impactful change, and with the additional support of leading-edge facilitation and coaching they are able to ensure the right combinations of performance, growth and wellbeing.

Learn more from Australia's leading change and leadership facilitator, visit: www.louise-gilbert.com

ACKNOWLEDGEMENTS

A LUNCHEON before one of Melbourne's lockdowns in 2021 is the best I can do in pinning down the day the seed of writing a book finally sprouted. I have Lesley Williams to thank for that wonderful lunch, her encouragement, and her support.

In truth, I was told by my book coaches, Kelly and Carolyn, that writing a book is in the re-writing. This has certainly been my experience as I've personally explored the tension and possibilities of looking after myself and my wellbeing, as well as my family's while growing myself and my business and maximising its performance from that 2021 lunch through to the most challenging year of my life in 2024.

One of my teachers in coaching psychology, Dr Michael Cavanagh, once said, 'We become who we are in connection with others,' and I think this book is an extension of the work my business has been doing and will continue to do, as well as the lessons

I'm learning in life, thanks to the communities and people who shape me.

In the last couple of years, I've had a crash course in neurodivergence, and I want to specifically thank Sandhya Menon and the broader lived experience community. I have never made so many 'friends' online before or gotten into such deep conversations in other communities.

My husband, Josh, gets the real behind-the-scenes view. Thank you for letting me infodump on you and for shaping our world so I can play to my strengths. And my parents, Jenny and Vince, who are a key part of our family system—thank you.

My best friend, Jess Biggs (Snow), whom I've known since kinder, has not only been the best sounding board and brainstorming partner but also introduced me to the work of Joan Lurie, who I'd also like to acknowledge. Joan has given me a new set of glasses.

Dr Travis Kemp has influenced me profoundly and held space for me in a way that words can't describe.

I've really benefited from the support, challenge and wisdom of Col Fink. Whip smart and caring, I value our relationship and your candour.

I conducted close to fifty interviews for this book, and I'm so grateful to everyone who shared their stories with me. As time went on and the writing unfolded, these wonderful stories inspired my writing, even if they didn't appear to feature.

To my friends, social media 'connections', and family who've cheered me on from the sidelines—

thank you for showing your interest and support. Working out loud for you has kept me accountable.

A huge thanks to you, the reader, for picking up this book and diving into these pages and practices with me. I'd love to hear how you go with them.

And finally, thank you to all of my clients. I created my business as a container to accelerate good change in the world, and every time we work together, we get to make work work for you.

ABOUT
THE AUTHOR

LOUISE GILBERT is the Director of *Louise Gilbert*. She is a speaker, coach, mentor and facilitator with a career in change spanning almost two decades. Louise has advised hundreds of Australia's top organisations and is Australia's leading expert in delivering team and leadership coaching within organisations that facilitates transformational outcomes for her clients.

After establishing a successful career as a senior manager in change strategy at the National Australia Bank, Louise established her own business to help leaders and teams to be the best they can be. She now works with both large and small organisations, including Coles, Ambulance Victoria, L'Oreal and local businesses in Melbourne and Sydney. Louise helps leaders manage change and guide teams to achieve excellence through her proven model known as the Three Pedals of Excellence.

Her mission is accelerating much-needed change in the world through business.

Louise's extensive list of qualifications include a Bachelor of Psychology and Management/Marketing from Monash University. She has also attended the Management Exchange Program at the Copenhagen Business School in Denmark, the Melbourne Accelerator Velocity Program and the Institute of Coaching and Consulting Psychology. At the last count, Louise had completed twenty-eight licences, certifications and short courses. She is also a qualified make-up artist and plays the piano.

Having been identified as neurodivergent late in life, Louise's coaching programs, workshops and presentations are designed for neurodivergent inclusion.

She is the daughter of an Australian mother and a Burmese father and lives in Melbourne with her husband and two children.

NOTES

NOTES

NOTES

NOTES

NOTES

NOTES

NOTES

NOTES

www.ingramcontent.com/pod-product-compliance
Lightning Source LLC
Chambersburg PA
CBHW030452210326
41597CB00013B/644